CRIC

O

THE GREEN

a celebration
of
Woodford Green Cricket Club

edited by
ARTHUR LINDFIELD
and
BILL NAISMITH

To Tony and Helen
Best wishes
Bill

WOODFORD GREEN
CRICKET CLUB

First published in 1999
by Woodford Green Cricket Club
3 The Terrace, Woodford Green, Essex IG8 0XS

Typeset by Country Setting, Kingsdown, Kent CT14 8ES
Printed in England by Intype London Ltd

A CIP record for this book
is available from the British Library

ISBN 0-9536178-0-7

Contents

Acknowledgements

THE EDITORS would like to thank all the following for their help with the compilation of this book: Don Coates; Jayant Desai; *The Guardian and Independent*; Geoffrey James; Stanley Hecquer Studios; Peter Lawrence, Chairman of the Woodford Historical Society; Andrew Naismith; Bob Provis; staff of Loughton Library; the landlords of *The Cricketers* and *The White Hart*; the Woodford Green Amenity Group (photographer, Peter French); Julia Lewis; Robert Palmer; John Smith-Pryor; Colin Smith-Pryor; Robin and Anne Wolstenholme.

Introduction

CRICKET ON THE GREEN is intended, at the end of the twentieth century, to celebrate Woodford's long association with cricket on the Green. It also covers the history of Woodford Green Cricket Club as far as we have been able to research it.

By its very nature as a village cricket club, operating for many years with the most basic facilities (first a small tent, then a larger one), the retention of records has been problematic. The stoppage of play during two world wars and the occasional sudden departure (for reasons unknown!) of a club officer in possession of club documents has meant that a lot of information has simply disappeared. Happily, however, *The Woodford Times* recorded the club's matches during the last quarter of the nineteenth century and the early twentieth century, as well as many of the club's social functions. Recent history is more complete.

Again, as is typical of village cricket clubs, Woodford Green C.C. makes no claim to having produced a Compton or a Botham. For this reason we have deliberately avoided the inclusion of repetitive details of statistics, scores and fixtures. Anybody interested in a week-by-week record of match scores is directed to past copies of *The Woodford Times* and *The Guardian.* It *is* possible, nevertheless, to gain great satisfaction from playing at any level of cricket, as we all know. A match winning or saving innings, a hat-trick or a good catch are never forgotten. The memories of club players attest vividly to this fact.

We are also conscious of what might be considered a vital omission. That is a detailed description of what really makes a village cricket club the unique institution that it is. This, of course, involves the 'characters' of the club. Most village cricketers are good-hearted, cheerful and friendly souls who are a delight to be with. But all cricket clubs also have their characters: the instantly recognisable 'types' – the batsman who is *never* out, the boring drinker, the ladykiller, the loud purveyor of unfunny jokes, the misery in the corner who has seen it all before and would never be seen to applaud a century. We have always had more than our fair share of characters, but our limited talent could never do them justice. We have preferred to let our worthy members speak for themselves – hence the 'Woodford Tales' and the evergreen anecdotes which intersperse the main chapters of our narrative.

We have tried to compile a book that describes the nature of village cricket by celebrating Woodford Green Cricket Club, which has played on the Green, opposite The Castle pub, for a great many years.

A.G.L. & B.N.

Spectators on the Green.

1

Early Days

WOODFORD GREEN Cricket Club has long claimed that its origins were established in the distant past. The year 1735 has been given as a starting point, and this date allowed for a grand celebration in 1985 to mark 250 years of cricket on the Green. Five local mayors were welcomed to a luncheon by the Corporation of London, together with the Essex 2nd XI who were to play on the Green that day. Unfortunately, rain prevented a ball being bowled and Woodford were denied the chance to host Steve Waugh, later to become the Australian captain, who came to play for Essex.

Cricket was certainly played on the Green in the early eighteenth century, as is shown in historical records of early cricket in Essex, but in the earliest days it is unlikely that 'clubs', as such, were involved. Mainly the matches were challenge games, sometimes played for high stakes. For example, *Berington's Evening Post*, in June 1732, announced a match to be played in Epping Forest between Essex and Hertfordshire for £50 (play or pay!), with the order that 'Wickets to be pitched at 1.00 precisely or forfeit half the money'. Another challenge match is recorded in *Cricket Quarterly*, Volume VII, to be played between Leyton and Woodford Green by The Green Man in Leyton. *The Daily Advertiser* of June 1755 announced a match between 'Hackney v. Woodford, 11-a-side. Stumps pitched by 1, to meet at the Nag's Head in Mare Street. Two matches to be played single-handed for ten guineas each.' Closer to home, the M.C.C. has confirmed that in 1786 'at the Cattle and Two Brewers at Woodford (a coaching-inn which

The Castle in Victorian times, showing the main highway from the City to Epping.

preceded The Castle pub) Woodford beat Chigwood (possibly Chigwell?) by 135 notches. It is highly unlikely that this was the *first* match played on the Green. In another match at Woodford, in 1795, the home team beat Highgate by 16 notches in a two innings game played for 100 guineas. The scores are given in H. T. Waghorn's *The Dawn of Cricket* – Woodford, 78 and 37; Highgate 43 and 56. This included 12 ducks and a great many innings of 7 or less. Furthermore, in 1761 the *General Evening Post* mentions a match between 22 of Essex and 8 of Dartford with 3 'given men' for £50-a-side at Woodford Row in Essex. Woodford Row is now the High Road, adjacent to the Green.

Other matches are recorded as being played in the early nineteenth century close to the Green. The 1808 Essex v. Homerton match (featuring the famed Lord Frederick Beauclerk) was certainly played, and Harold Hobson describes it as taking place on the Green in his novel *The Devil in Woodford Wells*, which is dealt with later in this book. *The Chelmsford Chronicle* records a match between Essex and the Aldgate Association on Woodford Wells Green, in front of Tom Rounding's house. The Essex team comprised 6 from Hornchurch, 2 from Waltham Abbey, 2 from Woodford and 1 from Abridge.

Cricket in Woodford was clearly a popular pastime in these early days, but was to prove fatal in one incident recorded by *The Brighton Examiner* of July, 1858, under the heading 'Awfully Sudden Death'. The circumstances were described as follows:

> It is with much regret we have to announce to our readers the sudden decease on Monday of Mr William Beedham under the following painful circumstances. It appears that the late gentleman had been away from Brighton about ten days on an excursion for recreation and health, and was at the establishment of Messrs Easton and Amos at Woodford in Essex with whom he was long acquainted, and whose men numbering about 300 had on Monday a holiday and were enjoying themselves in various ways. Mr Beedham went about twelve o'clock among a portion of the men who were playing cricket, and, taking the ball in his hand, said jocularly, 'Now I will show you how to bowl', and bowling knocked down the wicket. The ball was then thrown back to him which he caught, and which in the act of giving it another jerk suddenly fell back and died instantaneously. It is thought that the death was occasioned by a rupture of a blood-vessel in the head, but it was known he was suffering from disease of the heart.

Clearly, then, the tradition of bank holiday cricket in Woodford has a long tradition, however unfortunate for this overreaching visitor.

A degree of confusion surrounds the earliest history of cricket in Woodford because it was evidently played at a variety of venues, and certainly a 'Woodford' club played for some time near George Lane in South Woodford. Wanstead Cricket Club trace their origins to this same 'Woodford' club. There used to be a 'Woodford Wanderers', a 'Woodford Parkdale', a 'Woodford Thursday', a 'Woodford Green Tradesmen' and a 'Woodford College'. Also there were other grounds very close to the Green where cricket was played within living memory – for example, there used to be cricket pitches opposite the two hospitals close to the Green, Harts and The Jubilee, that have sadly been closed down. Because cricket is no longer played at these other venues, Woodford Green C.C. feels vindicated in claiming to represent the unbroken tradition of cricket in Woodford that stretches back to the early

An early picture of cricket on the Green, late nineteenth century, before the avenues of trees were planted. Note the 'crowd'.

eighteenth century, and to have played on the same ground for longer than any of our neighbouring clubs.

So what about the year 1735? This was fifty years before the French Revolution, when George II was on the throne, Robert Walpole was Britain's first Prime Minister and George Washington was three years old. In fact this date given for the beginning of the club derives from a story told by Mr Caesar Hoy who played for the Green for many years. He lived to a great age and claimed that he first played for the club at the age of fifteen in the year 1868, at which time the rules of cricket were well established. He said that his father played for the club before he first joined, and his grandfather, who died at the age of 96, commenced playing in the year 1785 'when Woodford Green C.C. was in its fiftieth year'. Caesar Hoy was a celebrated local character and his death was reported at some length in *The Woodford Times* in 1934, as his diamond wedding had been two years earlier. Below, he is seen pictured with a Woodford team of of the 1890s. It is surely one of these 'Hoys' who is recorded as playing for Woodford Green against The Royal Gunpowder Factory – on the Green – in August, 1869, the earliest date we have of the local newspaper.

Woodford Green Cricket Club in the 1890s. Caesar Hoy is seated second from right.

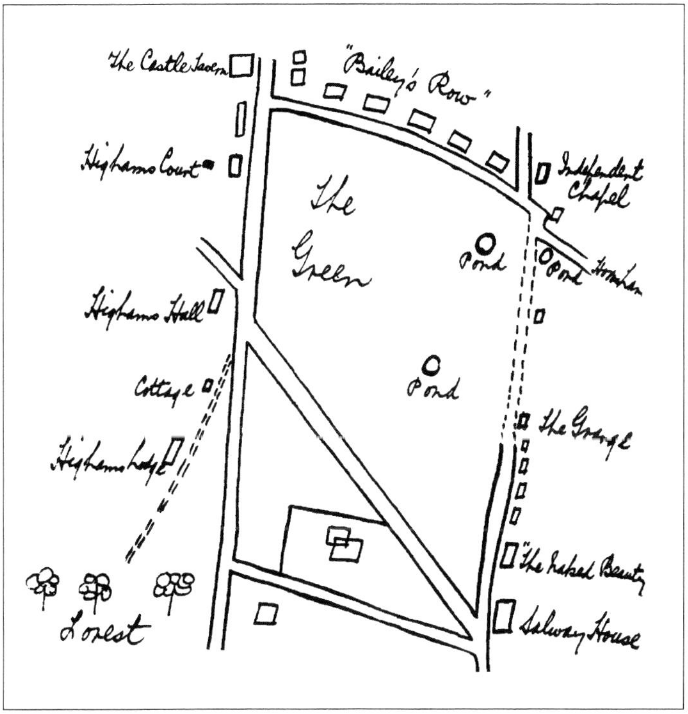

Impression of The Green and its neighbourhood, *c.* 1738 (from details kindly supplied by H. H. Stevens)

According to Hoy, matches in his day were arranged for eleven o'clock and terminated at six-thirty, the game being followed by a dinner at The Castle which was then the headquarters of the club. The brewers and distillers each annually contributed five guineas to the club funds. Visiting teams always arrived by stage coach, which was drawn up on the Green and used as a grandstand. Flags marked the boundaries, and the playing area was skirted by the three ponds that then existed on the Green. There were no poplars or chestnut trees surrounding the ground then, and The Terrace, which consisted of wooden cottages, was known as Bailey's Row. The playing pitch was prepared by first scything the grass and then watering by means of pails of water carried from the adjacent ponds; then the ground was levelled out with wooden rammers.

A.G.L. & B.N.

THE CAPTAIN'S TALE

Just as it is every schoolboy's dream to become the Captain of England's test side one day, it is the dream of many young club cricketers to become captain of their first eleven. Few, of course, achieve it, and most who do, live to regret it (*The paths of glory lead but to the grave*). And so it was with me.

There I was, a young ambitious cricketer, playing with modest success in the second eleven. After a match towards the end of the season, we were downing the obligatory pint or two in the Castle pub, when one of the seasoned players approached me and asked if I might be prepared to stand as captain next season, as he would like to propose me. I should add that our resident captain of some seasons, Ken Carpenter, who seemed set to see out his years unchallenged in that position, had mysteriously disappeared without word or trace. I made the mandatory protests of modesty before agreeing, and went home elated and eager to tell the wife of my new-found status and popularity.

The Annual General Meeting was held as usual on the last Sunday of February, in the Working Men's Club, as it was then known. (It is funny to recall in my short life span how the adjective 'working' has slumped from being heroic to derogatory.)

At the meeting the position of first team captain was put on hold, due to some transformations within the club that I shall refer to later. I was duly proposed and seconded as second team captain, and there being no other nominations, that should have been that, except the meeting was not unanimous in its acceptance. There was a dissenting voice: a voice, moreover, of no small influence.

Stan (The Man) Richardson had been a schoolteacher famed for his discipline, and was still feared by many an ex-pupil. After the war years he was the star player for Woodford Green, and even though no longer young, comfortably held a first team place. So that when Stan exclaimed, 'I object!', it had a profound effect on both the meeting and on me in particular. My heart sank. My dreams, so nearly realised, were being dashed. My disappointment was so profound that Stan's continuation did not register for some moments: 'I object because he is a first team player, and should not, therefore, become second team captain.'

Did he really say that? My self possession flared up for a moment – did I hear right? Perhaps he was not such a bad chap after all. Suddenly I saw not the tyrant of St. Barnabas Secondary Modern, but a man of avuncular wisdom. As you may imagine, this intervention threw the meeting into some confusion. The Officers huddled into groups of secret whispering, and the outcome, after due consultation, was that I was elected *first team captain* (a position I was to hold for some years). That night I could hardly sleep with the excitement and elation, and all the plans I had for the season ahead.

As the new season was almost upon us, a few ominous facts began to emerge. First there was the news that the quality core of the first team – Peter Howe, Stan Richardson, Alan Sheppard, Geoff Wood, Mike Curry and Peter Hassal – had decided to play Sundays only from now on. The reasons given were varied and plausible – 'The Garden', 'The Wife', 'Getting Old', 'Must support the Orient', etc. I recalled quite suddenly the huddled whispering of the officers at the A.G.M., and dark, dark thoughts entered my mind.

Next came the realisation that tea ladies had previously been supplied exclusively from the wives of these players, and that the member who had previously cut and marked the wicket was similarly indisposed, together with the lady scorer.

So my season of dreams began as a nightmare. I had a team of inexperienced youngsters, not many of whom showed signs of future greatness. Every Saturday morning I would rise with the lark, help make the sandwiches, spend an hour or so on the phone to find an eleventh player, then to the Green for pre-match duties. The first of these duties was to remove all the cow-pats with a shovel and wheelbarrow. In those days the cattle roamed freely and frequently across the Green, and usually found a way through our fence. I don't know if it was the lushness of our grass, or the straining to

penetrate our fence, but by the time those cows reached cover point they were clearly suffering chronic irritable bowel syndrome. On bad days I would remove three or four barrow loads of glutinous muck. After that came the cutting and marking of the strip for the afternoon match. I remember doubting that Ted Dexter or Colin Cowdrey had ever paid this kind of price for being captain. True, the Long Room at Lord's is famed for its huddled whispering, but never with such dark consequences as this.

And so, not surprisingly, our season started with us getting soundly thrashed by oppositions great and small. But by the end of that season, by dint of hours on the phone recruiting anyone I had ever met or heard of who could play cricket, and with the improvement of such young hopefuls as Trevor Spicer, Stevie Whyles and Richard Dodson, we became a respectable side. To the great relief of my poor wife I was no longer required to 'drink the fixture' every week. All might have been well from then on, but for the earlier imprudence of my youthful loins, which had brought about three sons. I should add a word of warning here to all young men who aspire to captaincy. If you have three sons, *don't do it*, or at least constrain your ambitions to home matches only.

South Woodford C.C. had planted a 'Memorial Willow Tree' at the edge of their boundary, and it was showing all the signs of maturing into a fine specimen. Unfortunately, a well meaning friend or uncle had seen fit to buy one of the boys a small saw for his birthday, and during the course of play came a childish shout of 'Timber!', and the tree was no more. I would not dare to suggest that the Captain of South Woodford C.C. was in any way an unreasonable man, but not even the most abject apologies, nor the continued filling of his glass could appease him. He made it plain that I was only welcome in future *minus sons*. Since my wife had by now been pressed into both scorer and tea lady, this was not an easy undertaking to give.

I really should have taken the saw away and broken it into small pieces, but the pleasure it so obviously gave them was difficult to resist – until that is, the visit to Nazeing Common C.C. Nazeing, a village green side, had been very resourceful and built a splendid new pavilion complete with bar and pool table. When we came in from fielding, someone noticed that the pool table was somewhat akimbo and one of its legs lay freshly felled on the floor. I was so distraught, I did the only thing a gentleman can, and ordered jugs of placatory bitter. The jugs continued to flow, but unfortunately, due to all the excitement, I forgot to pay my bar bill, and a very hostile letter was received by our club.

The saw having by now been destroyed, I approached our next away match with calm and confidence. Whitbread's, famed for its facilities and probably the best tea in England, was to be the venue. As usual we fielded first, and all was well, the boys being unusually quiet. As we came in to tea, I patted them affectionately and said, 'Good lads.' In the splendid tea room at Whitbread's, something was not quite right. There were plates, there were cups and even an urn of tea, but of sandwich and of cake, not a trace. Their captain summoned the tea ladies for explanation, and said it was not good enough. They protested their innocence, and swore it had all been laid out in the proper fashion.

With a sudden sinking feeling I realised that the boys had made themselves scarce and were nowhere to be seen. A lady spectator, rising from her deckchair, confirmed the worst. She had seen three small boys coming and going with sandwiches and cakes. For anyone who has never been in the position of explaining to twenty-two hungry cricketers that your sons have cleared the lot, leaving not even a crumb, please accept that it does not make for a happy day's cricket.

Of course one cannot physically shackle young children, and the constant threats of thrashing, skinning alive, plunging in boiling oil etc. had been too often repeated, and were received with a smile and 'Sorry Dad'. At Walthamstow C.C. we were fielding first and I was, therefore, beyond striking distance of the boys, when a great shriek went up. I looked across to see a group of people dancing about like dervishes and shouting and waving fists. It quickly became apparent that the boys had discovered a gallon can of pale blue paint (I have supported Oxford ever since), managed to prise it open, then climbed onto the roof of the pavilion and emptied the entire contents over the Walthamstow players and scorers in their line of deckchairs.

Now I am not suggesting that a sense of humour should be a prerequisite to captaincy, but I must say I was pretty disappointed that many of my fellow captains seemed to be without one. All these years later, whenever I visit one of those clubs (and others), I hastily look around in dread of spotting someone of a sufficient age to remember.

BRIAN PERRING

2

The Devil in Woodford Wells

The Devil in Woodford Wells is a novel published in 1946 by Harold Hobson, who was to become the leading theatre critic of *The Sunday Times* in the 1950s and 1960s. Its relevance to this volume of memories of the Green concerns a central preoccupation of the book, which is a cricket match played in 1808 between Woodford Wells and Homerton on what is, indisputably, our ground at Woodford Green. As such the novel has a curiosity value.

Curiosity is, perhaps, its major value, because in truth *The Devil in Woodford Wells* is a pretty dreadful hotchpotch of a novel. It is subtitled 'A Fantastic Novel', with 'fantastic' referring not to the quality of the story but to the supernatural element which makes it essentially a ghost story. Set partly in Woodford Wells/ Woodford Green (where the narrator John Mallard lives with his wife and daughter) and partly in London, where he works as a journalist and broadcaster, the novel traces Mallard's research into certain intriguing details of the cricket match which he has found recorded in Lillywhite's *M.C.C. Scores and Biographies*. It also concerns his relationship with a character called Enoch Soames who has, 'fantastically', made a Faustian pact with the Devil – sometime in the late nineteenth century – to remain alive and young. Soames, quite improbably, derives from a story by Max Beerbohm.

Mallard owes much, I suspect, to the character of the author, and the whole book is a piece of self-indulgent whimsy, peppered with leaden humour, that could not possibly find a publisher to-day. It is kept in the reserve section of the Woodford Library no doubt because of its title. There is some period detail that is interesting (the story occurs in 1941 during the blitz, and like Noël Coward's *Blithe Spirit* looks to fantasy to escape from more serious matters) and there is a fair amount of literary debate between Soames and Mallard. The novel is kept of its time by the narrator's tiresome paternalism and his references to friends as 'old fellow' and 'old man': his wife is 'old girl'. However, the main failing of the book is the total lack of a sustained and interesting story line.

This is a pity because a good story might have been made out of the cricket match, which featured Lord Frederick Beauclerk – arguably the best player of his time. Mallard, the narrator, was drawn to the match because 'it was played on the village green, now overlooked by a temperance hotel, at Woodford Wells, where I live, in Essex, a dozen miles north-east of London. It is the only great match I have ever heard of being played there. It is certainly the only match in Woodford Wells in which Beauclerk appeared (p. 35)'. Why Harold Hobson sets the match featuring Woodford Wells on the Green is never made clear, but there is no question about the venue – and this is the most fascinating aspect of the book.

Not just the temperance hotel (which used to be on the corner of Chingford Lane) is mentioned. Further evidence includes (p. 38):

> The road to Epping and Cambridge cuts along the west boundary of the green, and over the way there's the Girls' High School . . . also 'The Naked Lady', that is the house which stands at one corner of the green, at the edge of the trees, and looks diagonally across it towards the high-road. It's in the Queen Anne style, it's very old, and it used to be painted white.

Furthermore Hobson records 'a particularly fine avenue of poplars running along one side of the green, and a row of chestnuts opposite to it'. Clearly the Green acted as an inspiration to the writer because, as he says, 'his fancy was intrigued by the picture of a sunny village green, lined with elms, white figures gliding to and fro in silk shirts and stockings over the grass in the shadow of the church spire, with the monstrous menace of Napoleon just across the Channel lowering with doom and death' (p. 37). A similar menace was hovering over the Channel in 1941, when perhaps the Green at Woodford provided some domestic solace to Harold Hobson.

Hobson invents the notion that scores in the match were deliberately manipulated to send coded messages to the English forces abroad, and that there was mischief behind the game: 'That anything like treachery should be mixed up with the sacred game of cricket seemed to us an exquisitely daring notion'. Unfortunately the recent match-fixing allegations levelled at international players in the 1990s can easily be traced back to the early nineteenth century and probably before! The truth of the corrupted match is revealed by Lord Frederick Beauclerk to the narrator's ghostly friend Soames. According to the book they were now fellow residents in Hell. It is Soames who introduces the Devil to Woodford Wells. Believe that if you like.

Carr's Dictionary of Extra-ordinary English Cricketers describes the Reverend Lord Frederick Beauclerk, D.D., as:

Vicar of St. Albans, *c.*1820, great-grandson of King Charles II and Nell Gwynne and known in the Soho district as Fred Diamond Eye. This choleric man took his stand at the wicket wearing a scarlet sash and a white beaver and demonstrated his contempt for some bowlers by suspending a valuable gold watch from his middle stump. He is said to have been an unutterably dull preacher. B.N.

THE TEA LADY'S TALE

Some Notes for a Novice

Tea for 26, to be ready any time between four and five o'clock on Saturday, sounds straightforward. But is it? Finding people ready to commit to it is a seasonal battle for any cricket club, and no wonder.

Confronting each Tea Lady is the happy task of preparing sandwiches, with a range of fillings to suit all tastes and religious persuasions, together with the provision of assorted cakes and biscuits. Added to this is the expenditure of a considerable amount of time (by women with little to spare) in the supermarket queue and at the sink.

Preparing a cricket tea also opens the door to a series of compromises. These start with public embarrassment at the checkout, with a trolley filled with decadent cakes and sliced white bread, instead of trendy salad vegetables and healthy wholemeal loaves – try convincing sportsmen they'll like what is good for them! Next come the attempts at self justification when younger colleagues query the need for grown men to be fed like children at a party – 'Can't they bring their own?' and 'Why don't you go off and enjoy yourself if you have a free afternoon?' Finally there is the need to control the joyful response of 'No trouble, I enjoy it,' if that rare moment, a word of thanks from the opposition captain, or an offer of help with the washing up, is forthcoming.

The reality is that women of a certain age, usually those with a full-time job and a husband or son in one of the teams, can be persuaded to do their bit for the club during the season. The routine has worked for years.

A Typical Tea Day

The Shopping Confident about the fixture and the weather, the Tea Lady can purchase, or even make the components, in her own time – wise ones however will wait until the very last moment, in hope of being saved by a miraculous downpour. The practical and financial ramifications of a rained-off match are too elaborate to be gone into here. It should also be remembered that a Tea Lady should not expect to be re-imbursed for her pains until *after* the game, when match fees are duly collected and the captain can be reminded of his duty. There is an upper limit of expenditure, so woe betide anyone who carelessly overspends, in an attempt to provide a lavish tea. So don't ever try to compete with St. Margaretsbury's!

The Preparation An intense two-hour slog, combining bread with fillings and arranging selections of cakes in a tasteful array. Easy enough you will think, but most people prefer to do this in their own kitchen, making the transportation of everything to the pavilion something of a challenge. Once at the pavilion and whilst laying out all in readiness for the break, half-way through the match, the Tea Lady must also set up hot and cold drinks to be available. Everything should be provided in enough quantities to satisfy the single men in the teams who see this as their main sustenance for the weekend. Individual needs have to be catered for, too – Phil's pickle, Robin's squash, Paul's Dairylea Cheese, etc.

Novices who think that everything can be done in the pavilion kitchen soon learn, as they fight a losing battle with other people's children, stray dogs, aged camp followers wanting the 'gents' and bar habitués who want to conduct meandering conversations. And don't expect to have access to the sophisticated facilities of the bar (fridges, dish-washer etc.) because they will certainly be locked up come tea-time.

Tea-time With about five minutes notice the teams will leave the field and crowd in to eat. Players only should be served first, but there are always one or two who smuggle their children in or some sandwiches out to waiting families. Even before this the Tea Lady will have had to watch her provisions like a hawk, as various people find excuses to come in and gaze hungrily at the spread, determined to help themselves if they can. The complete contents of a plate of spring onions once disappeared into a breast pocket as the guilty party decided that nothing at all on the plate looked more convincing than the few stalks he'd left at first.

As the tea is poured, plates piled high are addressed. In fifteen minutes little is left and the captains are organising teams to continue the game. Then the Tea Lady can provide supporters with drinks and invite them in to pick over the remnants.

Washing-up A mountain of crockery to be washed and dried awaits. The efficient captain delegates some players to help with this if at all possible, but these reluctant helpers usually lose interest, so it is probably not until six o'clock, hours after the first sandwiches were made, that the marathon is drawing to a close.

Afterwards Having endured the critical eyes of other tea ladies – 'Did you make enough dear, there's not much left,' or 'There's a lot left over, I think you'll find not many people like fish' – the weary Tea Lady can hope for a gin and tonic from the captain, especially if his team is victorious, and eventually a cash settlement to cover her expenses. All that's left is to go home to her own chaotic kitchen and the delights of feeding her own hungry family. And, be sure, you can expect a cheerful phone call very soon – 'Are you free a week on Saturday by any chance?'

CLARE NAISMITH

3

The Victorian Era

WOODFORD GREEN Cricket Club flourished during the reign of Queen Victoria and cricket played on the Green was regularly reported in *The Woodford Times*.

In 1840 Woodford was a small village of less than five hundred houses – as indeed at that time was Ilford, whose population was to race ahead during the century. The Green presented a very different picture from that of to-day. With the possible exception of some trees along the hedgerow which separated it from Broomhill Walk (now Broomhill Road), it was a clear open space.

The first fine avenue of poplars was not planted until 1887 to commemorate the Jubilee of Queen Victoria, and the chestnut trees now bordering on the High Road were not planted until 1892 – the Local Board being responsible for planting the line from Knighton to Salway Hill with a view to enhancing the local recreation grounds.

There were two small ponds on the Green, one in the middle opposite Chingford Lane, and the other on the edge near the point where Fairfield Road now joins Broomhill Road. Opposite The Castle pub, instead of the shops and bank premises, there were some small cottages, and more houses and cottages stretched down The Terrace. The Police Station stood near the High Road facing the Green, and the site of the Congregational Church was then occupied by the Woodford Independent Chapel. The latter was demolished when the existing church was built in 1874.

By 1901 Woodford had grown to contain over two and a half thousand houses with a population of over eleven thousand people. As a suburb it was well known for its high proportion of the 'well-to-do', and its large number of very fine houses – positive mansions by to-day's standards.

There was unquestionably a very strong communal spirit in Woodford during the Victorian era which was recognised by the Local Board and maintained by many thriving churches in the area. Without television or even radio for diversion the incentive for joining clubs and societies was strong. Our cricket club was one of a vast array of opportunities. There were Liberal and Conservative Associations, a Horticultural Society, a Society for the development of Art and Industry, various Benefit and Building Societies, a Charity Organisation Society, Literary and Debating Clubs, a Working Men's Institute, Mutual Improvement Societies, a Temperance Society, a Young Men's Christian Association, Lawn Tennis and Lacrosse Clubs, Musical and Choral Societies, a School of Music, Weekly Penny Reading Entertainments during the winter, and a Dramatic Club.

The Green, which was now known for its cricket, also became the meeting and starting point of what was to become an exceptionally popular and spectacular annual event – the Woodford Cycle Meet. To quote details of one year, in 1890 1,300 cyclists representing 47 clubs met on the Green. Their ride took them to The Roebuck (in Buckhurst Hill) from where, in the evening, they progressed back to Woodford with their handlebars illuminated by lanterns – so that 'a very pretty sight was witnessed, the clubs coming up in double file, the captain riding alone at the head of each and the sub at the rear, all in perfect line'.

Despite this remarkably diverse range of activities there can be no question of how popular cricket was during this period, at all levels of play. The local editor of *The Woodford Times* could write in the 1880s:

Cricket has a tight hold on the English masses, for we question whether any game, amusement, entertainment, or pastime whatever, even with the added incentive of gambling, other than it could hold over 20,000 standers and sitters in a field for hours of intermittent sunshine and shower, as the match between the representatives of Surrey and Nottinghamshire at Kennington Oval this week did. It augurs well for the future of bat and ball that a struggle could evoke and sustain so keen an interest on its own pure sportsmanly merits. Long may the fame of our cricket stand spotless. Long may its unsurpassed popularity continue.

The keen interest was as strongly maintained on the village green as on the county ground, and cricket in the Woodford area developed widely in the last quarter of the century, with numerous clubs being established in line with the national enthusiasm. *The Woodford Times* could proudly boast in 1886 that:

Woodford is certainly not behind other suburban parishes in the interest it takes in England's national game. There are few places where more champions of the bat will be found than in our own parish. The facilities for practice which the open greens afford have done much to encourage a love of the game among boys and men alike.

And, in particular, 'Woodford Green Cricket Club supplies a need experienced by young men at the upper part of the parish to spend their evenings enjoying cricket's manly toil.'

By then Woodford Wells was in its twenty-second year and had become the dominant club in the area, with a splendid private ground in Monkham's Lane. Other local clubs such as South Woodford, Chingford, Buckhurst Hill and Wanstead began around this time. The birth of a new club always attracted much interest in the local press. The popularity of the game in the area is indicated by these developments, but no stronger proof can be offered than the fact that one H. Ekens, a professional cricketer, opened a sports shop next to the Woodford Green Union Church to sell equipment.

Woodford Green Cricket Club did well throughout the period, winning far more games than it lost. It is remarkable how much

Aerial view showing the proximity of Woodford Green and Woodford Wells (photo Peter Lawrence).

interest was shown in the club by *The Woodford Times*, which covered, in a weekly issue, not only local but national and international news sufficient to keep anybody reading for the whole week. (For those interested, bound copies are retained in Loughton Library). Over *sixty* clubs, mainly from the East End of London, are recorded as having played against the Green during the Victorian period and the matches were apparently very well attended. We can read regularly of 'the large number of spectators gathered on the Castle Green to watch the play'. Of this long list of opposing clubs only three have survived (South Woodford, Woodford Wells and Chingford). Others no doubt folded together with their employers – for example, 'Leathercloth Company', 'G.E.R. Wagon Dept.', 'London and India Docks' and 'Upton Tradesmen'.

Among the earliest recorded matches, from the late 1860s, two wins in the same week were reported:

> The second match was played on Monday last at Woodford, with the Royal Gunpowder Factory Club, Waltham Abbey. A goodly number of spectators assembled and at times the road was lined with vehicles. The fielding on both sides throughout the day was good. The ground is not in good condition, being very hard, consequently several players were rather severely cut and bruised. Woodford won, with nine wickets to spare. We append the score of the match and no further remarks will be needed, but trust that Woodford players will muster strongly for Saturday, against the Middlesex United, as it will probably be their severest test this season.

Woodford duly delivered, and won on the Castle Green.

> The batting of all of the players except in one or two instances on the side of Middlesex was excellent, and we understand that in this particular the club is surpassed by no amateur club round London.

The praise was enthusiastically in favour of Woodford Green C.C.

> The scores of Messrs. Lomas and Spicer deserve special mention for the good stand made and the masterly display of batting, and both were very warmly applauded. 86 runs were scored by the Woodford eleven, winning the game by 23 runs. The match was decidedly the best the Woodford Green Club has played this season, and taxed the utmost skill possessed by the players.

Club Cricket in Woodford

Teams with Woodford in their title,
but now defunct, include the following:

Woodford (George Lane)
Woodford Harts (The Green, opposite Links Road)
Woodford Thursday (Radley's Lane)
Woodford Bridge (Ashton Playing Fields)
Woodford Wanderers
Woodford Green Tradesmen
Woodford College
Woodford Parkdale

The following teams are still in existence:

Woodford Green (The Green)
Woodford Wells (Monkham's Lane)
South Woodford (Highfield Road)

The distinguishing feature of Victorian village club cricket as reflected in the reports of Woodford Green C.C. is the frequency of very low scores. Clearly the wickets and outfields were not comparable with today. Not only was a century by a player unheard of, but a century scored by a team was something of an achievement.

During the 1880s Woodford Green won the following matches by dismissing the opposition for less than fifty: Waverley (31), Bow Alberts (40), Ashley (39), Rangers (36) Leathercloth Company (37). Against Warner the Green scored 45, but dismissed the opposition for 37 with M. Wallace taking 8 for 13. But the Green also were capable of collapse. In 1892 the Green were dismissed by Chingford for 23; and in 1897, against Albemarle, they chased 114 and were all out for 26 (which included 7 ducks). In a match between Woodford Green and Roslin where the scores were 69 and 43 only three players reached double figures. Clearly there has been a great shift of power during the next century from the bowler to the batsman, although it should be emphasised that this is at village cricket level. In 1895 W. G. Grace was honoured by Gloucestershire for his hundredth century.

Another feature of cricket at this time was that often a match went through to a second innings (no doubt this was brought about by the low scoring that was usual) but in the event of these second innings being incomplete then the match was decided on first innings scores. Also it frequently happened that a team batting second would carry on well after reaching the opposition's score.

The club was recognised for its 'acquiring strength and increased solidity' towards the end of the century. The club's development can be traced in the context of games played against our neighbours Woodford Wells, who have played us annually since the 1860s. Clearly, the Wells were a stronger side, better equipped, with better players and a stronger fixture list. They also played on a much better wicket. Until the Second World War players from the Green – the 'village' club – regarded the Wells as 'superior', with all the connotations of that term. So matches between the clubs were the highlight of the season.

The progress of both clubs was well recorded in the press, but the emphasis was different. The Wells is regularly acknowledged as 'taking the lead' among local clubs. In 1890 they engaged a professional (Whitelaw) from Nottingham. Complaints were made that they rarely promoted second team talent, but recruited new blood from outside when anybody left. Their ambition was undoubted. The Green, on the other hand, was regularly reported for having great parties in The Castle.

Matches between the two clubs were always advertised and very well attended. This was a fixture always to 'excite much friendly interest in the neighbourhood', and when the Wells began to hold a 'cricket week' it was always the game against Woodford Green

Team photo of Woodford Green Cricket Club in 1891.

that attracted the most attention – drawing the largest crowd and being most fully reported. The 1886 report in *The Woodford Times* gives a clear indication of the relative strengths of the sides:

Woodford Wells won the toss and went to the wickets. Runs came slowly at first, the bowling being straight and the fielding smart. Later on Erlebach (58) and Wilson (23) got set and hit freely. By the time the last wicket fell 176 runs had been scored. The bowling of the Woodford Green Club was exceedingly good throughout. They had some hard work to do in the field, but did not show any sign of flagging. At the wickets Grove (32) and W. Griggs (17) made a good stand in their first innings playing with much judgement. In the second innings some good batting was shown by Martin (20) and Carter (14). Notwithstanding all the efforts of the Woodford Green men their opponents proved too strong for them winning by an innings and 12 runs.

Woodford Wells 176
Woodford Green 87 and 73

This pattern has been regularly repeated over the years, but the tide has sometimes turned. Woodford Green played most competently in their normal weekly fixtures, which might not be said of the Wells. Three years after the above report, in 1889, Woodford Green played 23 matches, won 15, lost 6 and drew 2. The Wells won only 3. In that year A. Grove topped the batting averages with 17 from 22 innings, and M. Wallace topped the bowling with 45 wickets at an average of 3.6.

Woodford Green would seem to have had a quality side in the 1890s, and eventually managed to defeat the Wells, on August Bank Holiday 1893, before 200 spectators. When time permitted a game to go through to a second innings it was the first innings score which determined the result, and it was reported that 'for the first time during many years Woodford Green won on the first innings' – the scores being 82 to the Green against 70 for the Wells. The game was clearly a triumph for the Smiths. H. Smith scored 22 and took 9 wickets; J. Smith scored 18 and took 2 wickets. The match was 12-a-side. The Green won again in 1895 when Gatcum bowled finely to take 8 for 34 and Saunders (33) and Smith (32) batted well. It is unlikely that the Green fielded a stronger side in any of their earlier years than they did in the last decade of the century.

Reference is frequently made throughout the Victorian period to the friendly socialising of the Woodford Green Cricket Club, who engaged in much sociable eating, drinking, singing and smoking in addition to playing cricket: a tradition that happily continues to the present day. Many opportunities were found to celebrate socially, and the club was not shy about reporting these feasts. Strangely enough, no other club in the area made report of any social events to anything like the same extent. We can read in *The Woodford Times* that 'at the close of the game the players adjourned to the Castle Hotel, where they partook of an excellent tea, served by the host, Mr Honey', and 'A capital luncheon was enjoyed at the Leathern Bottle after a very enjoyable day'.

Following an Annual General Meeting, 'a smoking concert took place when capital songs were rendered by several members', and 'about thirty members and friends sat down to a capital meat tea at the Castle Hotel' – and so on and on. These splendid occasions for the club were reported alongside news of Jack the Ripper's pursuit in London of 'sin's soiled sisters', the arrest of Oscar Wilde, and the return of the British army from the Sudan.

A variety of games and activities were arranged purely to enhance the club spirit, and complemented the weekly competition from visiting clubs. The close of season was invariably marked by a special game, after which the club would enjoy their celebratory tea. Sometimes the married men would play the bachelors of the club (the bachelors winning more often than not). Sometimes the captain would put out a team against the vice-captain. In 1884 this match ended in a tie – scores being 31 and 39 against 34 and 36 – which was either exciting or a fix.

Towards the end of the century the club went on an annual outing to Blackmore, with players and friends travelling together in a brake. A two-innings match was followed by the inevitable 'capital luncheon' before the party returned to Woodford after what can be imagined to be the perfect day out.

Annual General Meetings of the club were always reported in the press and again the good spirit of the members was a key feature, with much congratulation being offered to the officers for their managing the club in a successful manner. Prizes were given to the outstanding players, including a bat and a mounted ball to the outstanding batsman and bowler and sometimes a silver mounted briar pipe in a case and a silver mounted cigarette holder in a case for the runners-up.

The jollity that has always been a part of the club did not distract from the seriousness of the play on the Green, for the club entertained a large number of teams during the Victorian period and more often than not sent them home defeated. An unfair result did not go unmentioned, as we can see from this report of a game against Leytonstone Atlas in 1886:

> A very exciting game was played on the Castle Green on Saturday last between these clubs resulting in favour of the latter by 3 runs. The home team would have won by 2 runs had not their opponent's umpire ruled against a ball being cleverly caught by W. Griggs close to the ground.

Does anything ever change? First innings scores were: Woodford Green 23; Atlas 26.

Captain Griggs' annoyance remains in print forever. So does the pain of one A. Willet, a visitor to the Green with Upton Tradesmen, who is reported as receiving 'a nasty hit in the face by the ball'. This is one of the rare indications of what must have been a really appalling wicket to play on, judging by the low-scoring matches of the time. However, Mr Willet would appear to have got off lightly compared with another cricket victim whose demise was reported on the same day: 'William Scotton, a well-known Nottinghamshire professional and ex-test player, gave what he considered to be a wrong umpiring decision: the fact obsessed him so much that he cut his own throat.' To captain Griggs of Woodford (and so many batsman in future years) it must have happened to the wrong umpire. A further interesting detail is reported in the same year, when a team called 'Early Closers' from Putney got lost on their way to Woodford while travelling in a brake. Perhaps they didn't close early enough? When they finally turned up they lost by 128 to 119 runs. A.G.L./B.N.

THE SCORER'S TALE

As a female in a cricketing family I was aware from an early age that I would never play for the local team. This revelation did not dissuade me from following another path, that of the scorer.

Although only fourteen years old, I was confident it was a job I could do. If various team members could do it, playing musical deck-chairs between padding up and changing the score board, I reckoned they were lucky to have me! A willing member of the team, albeit female, I was willing to sit for five hours on a hard bench armed with my full equipment of sharpened and coloured pencils.

What I was soon to discover was that it didn't matter what sex, age or capability I offered. When I was given the scorebook I became invisible.

I was surrounded by men who might have known better! The language was colourful, the shouting ear-piercing. What I wasn't used to, however, was the unzipping of trousers, hands disappearing, holding some strange object, and a shaking and kicking of legs in a sideways fashion. Was this some kind of ritual dance?

Being too embarrassed to acknowledge what was going on around me, I just sat and blushed and carried on with *my* job in hand.

I was of more use to the opposition. They talked to me. I knew the names of bowlers, catchers and all sorts of useful information – nearest sweet-shop, toilets, what time the bar opened . . .

What I was soon to discover was how disloyal, sitting amongst the opposition, I could become. 'Bowler's name?' I gave it. Yes, it was my Dad, but I wasn't prepared to admit I was related to him. Howls of laughter – 'What does he think he's doing?'

My Dad took a three-step run up and launched the ball into the air – a full six-seconds donkey drop. When I heard the clink of the bails I smiled to myself and proudly filled in, under scorer's name – Jacqui Lindfield.

JACQUI BOYNTON (NÉE LINDFIELD)

4

The Selection Committee

IN 1988 Woodford Green Cricket Club mounted a cabaret in aid of charity, performed at Old Loughtonians Hockey Club, which featured an impressively large cast who were able to display a range of hitherto undiscovered talent for the stage. All captains of a village cricket club should easily recognise and sympathise with the problems confronted by the fantasy 'selection committee' which met that night.

Cast

Chairman
Bob

Captains
John
Terry
Robin
Alva

Sound: theme tune for Test Match Special.

All enter carrying pint glasses, half full, and sit.

BOB Right, we've got a lot of teams to pick for next weekend, and I don't want the trouble we got into last week. So, how are we fixed?

JOHN There's my team. (*Placing sheet on table.*)

TERRY There's my team. (*Ditto.*)

ROBIN There's my team. (*Ditto.*)

ALVA There's my team. (*Ditto.*)

BOB Fantastic. I don't believe it. That's marvellous. Must be a record. Let's have a drink.

All glasses are replenished from a jug, amidst much mutual congratulation, until . . .

TERRY Wait a minute. (*To Robin.*) You've got Tony down for Saturday.

ROBIN I know I've got Tony down for Saturday.

TERRY He's not available on Saturday.

ROBIN He told me he was available.

JOHN Yes. He's available on Saturday. He told me.

TERRY He's not available.

BOB Better ring him up and ask.

TERRY (*on phone*) Hello Tony. How's it going? You OK for Saturday? You are? Great. See you, Tony. (*To committee.*) He's available Saturday.

ROBIN I told you he was available Saturday.

BOB Right. So Tony knows he's playing on Saturday?

TERRY No. He doesn't know he's playing. He just told me he was available.

ROBIN Well ring him up and tell him he's picked for me.

TERRY (*on phone*) Hello Tony. How's it going? OK for the Seconds on Saturday? Great. On the Green. One-thirty meet, alright? See you, Tony.

BOB He's OK for Saturday then?

TERRY Yes. I told him half past one on the Green.

BOB But it's not on the Green on Saturday.

TERRY It is on the Green. Look in the fixture card.

JOHN No. It's been moved to Chigwell.

ROBIN What do you mean, it's been moved to Chigwell?

BOB He's right. All the home games in June have been moved to Chigwell.

ROBIN What for?

BOB The groundsman says the square is getting too dry. So we're going to play at Chigwell.

ROBIN But he cancelled all the home games in May because it was too wet.

BOB I know. But if we keep playing on the Green in the Summer, it won't be fit for Boxing Day. We take a lot of money on Boxing Day.

ROBIN So, tell Tony it's Chigwell on Saturday.

TERRY (*on phone*) Hello Tony. How's it going? Sorry Tony, it's Chigwell on Saturday, not the Green. OK? See you Tony.

JOHN Tony's playing for me on Sunday as well.

ROBIN No. Tony's definitely not available on Sunday.

JOHN Yes he is. He told me last week.

TERRY No. Tony's only playing Saturdays.

JOHN No, no, no. He said he was OK for Sunday.

BOB Better ask him. Give him a call.

TERRY (*on phone*) Hello Tony. How's it going? You available on Sunday, Tony? Great. See you Tony. (*To committee.*) He is available Sunday.

JOHN I told you he was available. (*On phone.*) Hello Tony.

How's it going? Great. You're playing for me on Sunday, OK? It's at Snaresbrook, but they've changed their captain. Can't be as bad as last time. See you, Tony.

TERRY (*to Robin*) Just a minute. You've got Don Coates. He's down to play for me.

ROBIN No, no, no. I told him on Saturday he was playing for me.

JOHN Well, let's be fair, Don's a second team player.

TERRY No he's not, he's a third team player.

ROBIN He's a second team player. Look what he scored last year.

A heated discussion ensues regarding Don's expertise with the bat.

BOB (*banging table with a large mallet*) Order, order. Let's have a bit of sense in this selection.

ALVA I've picked him myself for the Firsts.

Silence.

BOB That means Don's down for three teams on Saturday.

TERRY And me on Sunday.

ROBIN And me on Sunday.

JOHN Don's not available on Sunday. He's got the kids.

ROBIN Well if Don's not available on Sunday, I'll have Tony.

TERRY But I need a batsman for my side.

ROBIN What do you mean, you need a batsman? Your team's full of batsmen.

TERRY Batsmen! Look at the list. How many of them can bat?

There follows a heated discussion regarding the poor performances of all named players.

BOB (*banging the table*) Alright, let Tony play for Robin. Now what about teas for Chigwell on Saturday?

ROBIN If Tony's playing, Deb will do them.

TERRY No. Deb won't do teas any more.

BOB What do you mean, she won't do teas? Why won't she?

TERRY Because of what was said.

ROBIN What was said?

JOHN Yes. What was said?

An embarrassed and fascinated silence awaits an answer.

TERRY Well. I don't like to say.

BOB But we're the committee. We've got to know these things.

TERRY Well, I did hear somebody say that the sandwiches were too small.

ROBIN No, no. It's because she started using paper plates.

TERRY And there wasn't any orange juice.

ROBIN Well, I can't do without orange juice. There's got to be orange juice.

BOB I heard somebody say there wasn't a sign of a cherry in the cherry cake.

TERRY And, what's more, the players had to serve themselves.

There is general consternation at news of this apostasy.

TERRY Anyway, she won't do teas. Tony says so.

ROBIN I'll ask her. (*On phone.*) Hello Debbie. How's it going? Can you possibly do me a favour? Is there any chance you might do teas for me on Saturday? Oh. You're going to a wedding. That's nice. Does Tony know? Only he's playing for me on Saturday. (*Pause.*) I see, Deb. Have a nice time. (*To committee.*) Tony's not available this weekend. He forgot about a wedding.

BOB Let's start again then. If Tony's not available we could ask Eric Beck.

TERRY No, he's playing for the Woodcutters.

BOB John Bernard?

TERRY No. He's playing for Old Loughtonians.

BOB Brian Hough?

TERRY No. He's playing for Wanstead.

The meeting continues forever, but is drowned out by the theme music and the lights fade.

BILL NAISMITH

THE DEBUTANT'S TALE

At last the call came – 'Castle pub at one o'clock Saturday.' I was relieved. It had been two weeks since my colleague had given the Woodford Green captain my name and phone number, and after a three-year lay-off I was keen to start playing again. I also thought it would be a good way of meeting some new people after moving into the area.

I was eager to make a good impression as the club obviously had plenty of players to choose from. After all, why wait three weeks to contact me? I arrived early and searched all the bars and saw no-one who remotely looked like a cricketer. Still, I was early. One o'clock came and still no sign: a mild sense of concern. Did he mean meet at one or leave at one? Either way I couldn't have missed them, surely? Perhaps I'd misunderstood and the match was to start at one and they had given up waiting.

I did another trawl and to my great relief a man who was obviously a cricketer appeared. He was small and rather dapper with a weather-beaten face – I could just visualise him crouching behind the stumps and neatly taking the ball down the legside and bringing his hand back just far enough to clip one of the bails off. He was probably a stylish opening bat as well. I approached with some confidence: 'Excuse me, do you have anything to do with the cricket club?' He looked startled and glanced around to make sure it was he I was talking to before muttering that he wasn't. He made me feel that I had accused him of something rather unsavoury but he wasn't going to make an issue of it. I apologised and took stock.

I'd been in the pub for what seemed like an eternity and either had to leave or buy something. A dilemma. What to order? Assuming he was going to arrive eventually, what if my new captain disapproved of drinking before the match? I decided to buy half of bitter. If necessary I'd pass it off as shandy – surely he wouldn't object to that.

Suddenly the place was full of men with cricket paraphernalia and the sound of large men noisily ordering pints. They had arrived. A genial man approached me. 'Are you Dave? Sorry I'm late.' I could have hugged him I was so relieved.

We were changing, and the captain called across to me: 'What do you do Dave?' 'I bat a bit'. 'Good. Get your pads on – number three, OK?' I gulped. I hadn't touched a bat for three seasons and felt out of touch but it seemed wimpish to ask to go in lower down the order. I was soon in. I could barely lay a bat on the ball and when I made any sort of decent contact it seemed to go straight to a fielder. By tea we had struggled to just over a hundred and I was amazed to learn that I had scored fifty.

It was surely not going to be enough to win. We got a few wickets but the runs were mounting up. A wicket fell and in came a left-hander who seemed in a hurry. It was as if he had remembered where he had left his bike and wanted to get back to it before his wife saw it. Crash! Four. Bang! Six. Wallop! Another six. We were doomed. At the other end, fortunately, wickets were falling and we had a chance if we could keep the slogger away from the strike.

Then disaster. We had the last man in but let him get a single. Four runs to win. Our man decided to win the game in style. The ball soared over the bowler's head. A certain six. Long on stood right on the boundary, apparently transfixed, and just as the ball neared him raised a languid arm – the way goal keepers do to shepherd a ball over the bar. The match was over but where was the ball? Suddenly the fielder gestured nonchalantly with his hand. The ball was in it. It was the best catch I'd ever seen. Welcome to the Green.

I knew I'd done well, so I was hopeful of an invitation to play the following week in spite of the obviously wide choice of demon players available to the captain. A lad approached and asked for money. 'Can you play next week?' 'Yes, if there's a place.'

The captain appeared. 'Of course there's a place after an innings like that. I'd have picked you two weeks ago but I lost your number. It was only when my missus found the piece of paper as she was hanging my flannels out to dry that I knew how to get in touch. Luckily I could just still read the number.'

I felt I was 'in', and barring a couple of scrapes along the way that's the way it's been ever since.

DAVE ROWLANDS

5

The Twentieth Century

Club records, including score books and minutes of meetings, have disappeared for the early part of the century, and so we are entirely dependent on newspaper reports for details of the club's activities, and these are limited. Happily and fortunately, however, players who joined the club in the late thirties are still alive and remember pre- and post-war cricket on the Green. Again, *The Woodford Times* has proved invaluable, and a small early history, *Two Centuries of Cricket at Woodford Green*, published in 1952, details a number of players by name, but these really are ghosts of the past. Frequently the early booklet lets us down with the claim, 'These people are too well known for their exploits to be recorded here.'

However a pattern emerges of regular play, home and away, of great enthusiasm for the club, of hard work by the members and of regular and successful social gatherings. Reports of matches on the Green consistently describe them as 'pleasant', 'very interesting' and 'very enjoyable'.

The Annual General Meeting of 1900 heard the announcement: 'The teams selected to play shall be posted up in *The Castle* where all can see them' – which certainly implies that players in those days were frequent visitors to the local pub; they had to be, if they wanted to play. Apart from a period (1905–1924) when the club's headquarters were Woodford Green Men's Club, *The Castle* was the main base of the club before our first permanent pavilion was built in the 1950s.

Incidental events during the early years include the abandonment of League Cricket in 1903 (which the club had been experimenting with) because of the dislike of the 'cut-throat' League spirit. It is to be noted that the club resisted joining a League for as long as possible in the modern period – for the same reason – and an argument against it still persists. Also the club amalgamated with (or absorbed) players from other clubs who had become insolvent. Firstly, in 1902, Woodford United joined us.

Soon after the beginning of the Second World War, Horn Lane C.C., run by the air raid wardens of the ARP, joined up with W.G.C.C. players who had not been called up for the armed forces. Later we gained some excellent players when both Ashley and Harold Hill folded. In 1923 a Tennis Section was started – playing for four years at the junction of Horn Lane and Grosvenor Gardens, before houses were built on the land. Also a Women's Cricket Team represented the club for some time in the late twenties.

Gentlemen versus Ladies on the Green in the 1920s.

FIXTURES 1952 SEASON

1st Eleven

Apl.	26.	H.	Married v Single
May	3.	A.	A.B.R.A.C.
	10.	H.	Old Heronians
	17.	A.	East Ham Corinths.
	24.	H.	Eton Manor
	31.	A.	Eton Mission
June	2.	H.	Mansfield House
	7.	H.	Downshall
	14.	A.	Howards Sports
	21.	H.	Woodlands
	28.	A.	Langite
July	5.	H.	E. W'stow Liberals
	12.	A.	Eton Manor
July	19.	H.	Marshalls
	26.	A.	Downshall
Aug.	2.	H.	East Ham Corinths.
	4.	A.	Woodford Wells
	9.	A.	Woodlands
	16.	H.	Langite
	23.	A.	Old Highburians
	30.	H.	Howards
Sep.	6.	A.	E. W'stow Liberals
	13.	H.	Old Highburians
	20.	H.	Hambro's Bank
	27.	H.	Eton Mission

2nd Eleven

Apl.	26.	H.	Married v Single
May	3.	H.	Kensonians
	10.	A.	Allnutts
	17.	H.	Roding Valley
	24.	A.	Mann Crossman 2nd's
	31.	H.	East Ham Baptist
June	2.	A.	R.A.F.A.R.N.O.
	7.	A.	Wallace & Wallace
	14.	A.	E. Ham Town 2nd's
	21.	A.	British Railways
	28.	H.	Wallace & Wallace
July	5.	A.	Old Plaistovians
July	12.	H.	Mann Crossman 2nd's
	19.	A.	Roding Valley
	26.	H.	Old Heronians 2nd's
Aug.	2.	A.	East Ham Baptist
	4.	H.	R.A.F.A.R.N.O.
	9.	H.	British Railways
	16.	A.	Kensonians
	23.	H.	Allnutts
	30.	A.	E. Ham Town 2nd XI
Sep.	6.	H.	Old Plaistovians
	13.	A.	Old Heronians 2nd's

Sunday Eleven (all away fixtures)

May	11.	Marshalls C.C.
	18.	Enfield Cables
	25.	Romford United Services
June	1.	
	8.	Plaistow Police
	15.	Peel Institute
	22.	Bishops Stortford
	29.	
July	6.	Buck & Hickman
	13.	Mansfield House
July	20.	Mann Crossman 1st XI
	27.	Old Heronians 1st XI
Aug.	3.	
	10.	Peel Institute
	17.	Hambro's Bank
	24.	Kearley & Tonge
	31.	B.D.V. (Rayleigh)
Sep.	7.	Sawbridgeworth
	14.	Buck & Hickman
	21.	Plaistow Police
	28.	South Woodford

Cricket on the Green before the First World War.

A striking feature of all the matches played up to and around the Second World War is the fantastic turnover of what must be regarded as small clubs, many of which were linked to places of employment. Woodford Green 1st XI played a regular 17 to 23 matches a season, but against ever-changing opposition.

It is, perhaps, a startling fact that of more than *forty* different clubs that our 1st, 2nd and Sunday XIs played in 1952 (according to the fixture list from nearly 50 years ago reproduced opposite), only *four* are included in our current fixture list (these being Eton Manor, Roding Valley, South Woodford and Woodford Wells).

Three conclusions emerge from this fact and from the results recorded. Firstly, it must be admitted, a number of clubs may have dropped us because of the poor state of the outfield on the Green. Old photographs show the many paths criss-crossing the Green very close to the playing area, and everybody used to complain about them. Indeed, as long ago as 1930, the Council erected barriers of chestnut fencing to try to prevent people creating more of these paths.

Secondly, the large number of clubs associated with employers must have folded when such companies went out of business. Thirdly, and most significantly, the regular inclusion of new opposition must have led, inevitably, to some incredible mismatches (God help the Fixture Secretary who, in all innocence, sends out a weak team against an unknown demon bowler!) Scores often reflect a very uneven contest.

Furthermore, ignorance of the many teams we played during the century makes assessment of the performances very difficult. As in earlier years it appears that the bowlers dominated, and in many matches a particular bowler would seem to have been unplayable. We can't tell whether he was brilliant, whether the opposition were inept, or whether the pitch was impossible to deal

---

Below and opposite page, top: the problem of paths on the Green.
Opposite page, bottom: Woodford Green Cricket Club in 1921.

with. In one match (in 1927) R. Burton took 7 for 6 and 7 for 22; in another (1931) Babs Sansom took 6 for 8 and 7 for 18; in 1931 also Burton took 8 for 9; S. Smith in 1933 took 8 for 30 (5 in 10 balls including a hat-trick); and in 1939 Rutherford took 6 for 8; later we can read of R. Groves taking 7 for 7. These are outstanding figures, and there are many more recorded bowling heroics, but generally scoring was not high.

There were, of course, exceptions. In one match against Downsell Old Boys C.C., played at Fairlop, Woodford Green followed the home side's total of 121 all out with a unique 210 for no wickets: A. Grimshaw carried his bat for exactly 100 not out, and R. J. Wood was undefeated with 110. There were no extras.

To keep things in perspective it is always salutary to follow Woodford Green's progress in their annual match against their illustrious neighbours Woodford Wells. These games always attracted detailed reports and, invariably, a sizeable crowd arrived at Monkham's in eager expectation on Bank Holiday Mondays. Woodford Green usually lost these games, having first put up a noble fight, especially in the field.

It appears that little mercy was shown by the Wells, the home team, who could always draw on superior players, who had a stronger fixture list and who were used to playing on a good wicket. Two results were humiliating. In 1923 the Wells scored 299 to the Green's 89; and in 1924, under the heading 'Village Green Vanquished' we read of the Wells having scored 365 to the Green's 45.

Great joy was registered when the Green won after many years, in 1921, when the Green scored 195 before dismissing the Wells for 114. Walter Smith, who was really an outstanding batsman for Woodford Green for some years, scored 85. It is darkly rumoured that the Wells were playing another important match that same

AT LAST!

WOODFORD GREEN defeated local rivals Woodford Wells in the annual derby match on Sunday—for the first time since 1921.

After the game Woodford Green captain Clive De Boer said: "These matches are always played in a tense atmosphere, but this game seemed to be even more tense than usual. I think that is why the scoring was so low."

Wells, put in to bat, found themselves in trouble against Green pacemen Perring (3-25) and Dobson (4-32) and at lunch were 70-6.

In three overs after the interval Wells added only eight runs for the loss of their final four wickets. Chumbley ended with the impressive return of 3-3 in two overs.

Green started their innings cautiously and lost several batsmen cheaply to bowlers Bone (3-16) and Rogers (5-25). Chumbley was the mainstay of the innings scoring 49 runs before throwing his wicket away trying to reach his 50.

With Chumbley dismissed at 78-6, Wells gained a new lease of life and took three more wickets for no score. At this point a draw looked the most likely result until Dobson prodded the vital run needed for victory.

After the match a member of the victorious 1921 Woodford Green side, Mr C. Samson, celebrated with the jubilant 1972 players.

WOODFORD WELLS: Offord c Smith b Dobson 6, Sanford c Smith b Perring 8, Rogers c Smith b Dobson 6, Irwin c Beck b Dobson 19, Dunston lbw b Perring 0, Caffrey b Chumbley 1, Roberts b Dobson 7, Bone b Perring 10, Foxall c Wood b Chumbley 2, Ayres b Chumbley 1, Goodwin not out 0, extras 18; **Total 78.** Bowling: Dobson 4-32, Perring 3-25, Chumbley 3-3.

WOODFORD GREEN: Wood c Caffey b Ayres 9, De Boer b Bone 1, Chumbley b Rogers 49, Andrews b Rogers 2, Perring lbw b Rogers 0, Beck b Rogers 1, Smith lbw b Bone 9, Howe b Rogers 4, North b Bone 0, Dobson not out 1, Hassall not out 0, extras 3. **Total 79-9.** Bowling: Bone 3-16, Rogers 5-25.

day, but a win is always a win! As the above clipping testifies, Woodford Green had to wait until 1972 for their next victory,

We have noted the low scoring that was a feature of nineteenth-century village cricket, but this hardly compares with Woodford Green's dismissal of the L.N.E.R. Wagon Department for 14 in 1923 or – wait for it – 'Woodcutters' for a grand total of 8 in 1931. Pride of place in the humiliation stakes, however, is given to our own side, Woodford Green C.C., who, against Sawbridgeworth in 1924 managed to reach the magnificent total of 6 all out! To add immortality to insult we are prepared to name them here – and serve them right:

Bright	0
Gilbey, G.	0
James	0
Barrett, E.	1
Muller, J.	0
Gregory, S.	1
Heywood, H.	1
Charlwood, S.	3
Walls, J.	0
Reynolds, J.	0
Oliver, F.	0
Total	6

The Green managed to advance to 28 all out in the second innings, but lost to Sawbridgeworth's score of 128. Of course, this was far from a typical score, and it is good to record the words of 'Argus' reporting yet another W.G.C.C. annual dinner in the thirties in his column *Around and About Woodford* published on 1 April 1938.

In fair weather and foul the Green Club has carried on for more than two hundred years and is, if anything, more an integral part of the life of Woodford than ever before. As mentioned during the evening the essential feature of the club's existence is that the players enjoy the game and if a mere spectator can add his quota, that goes for the onlookers as well.

With no pretensions to classic fame, the Green members have consistently played their best, and if we have seen them lose many matches in the past it has always been with the knowledge that they have been good losers.

In the twenties the playing was dominated by Wally Smith, both with bat and ball (top of both in 1924, averaging 27 with bat and 7.00 with ball), and by R.J.Smith and R.J. Wood and M. Wood (averaging 44 in 1927, having scored 666 runs in 17 innings – the next best average was 10). They stand out in the averages, and in match reports. Smiths were also dominant in the thirties, during which both A. Smith and S.J. Smith topped the averages at times. Post-war cricket on the Green and the progress of the club are well documented in minutes of club committee meetings, in detailed averages and statistics of matches played by all teams, and in regular reports in the local paper. Committee minutes, recording the business of the club on a monthly basis are, by definition, extremely repetitive. They are concerned with finances and fixtures, ground and equipment, membership and officers' reports. Minutes of meetings do show, nevertheless, how quickly time passes and how removed we are from the past.

The post-war club minutes remind us that members were still being called-up for the forces and that people were expected to be able to live on £2 a week. But as the minutes record only the decisions of the committee, we are left with some tantalising questions. Who asked for 'sweepstakes' to be stopped? And what was the spectator doing to disturb a match? Here are some details from club minutes of the post-war decade:

- 14 July 1950 Service members are not required to pay subscriptions but while on leave are entitled to play at a charge of 2/6d per game.

- 20 October 1950 Cost of publishing a History of the Club – £100 for 500 copies (20p each).

- 6 June 1951 Insurance policy taken out covering members receiving injuries whilst playing. The benefits include: £2 per week for 52 weeks if unable to work; £200 for death or total disablement; £100 for partial disablement.

- 30 November 1951 It was proposed that the resolution passed at the A.G.M. of 19 November 1948, 'That no sweepstakes be held in future,' be rescinded.

- 7 March 1952 A letter from Mr Winston Churchill was read stating that he was unable to be present at our annual dinner.

- 6 August 1953 Mr Powter reported the disturbance by a spectator during the match with Rafarno C.C. and it was agreed that a letter of apology be sent.

- 18 November 1955 Thanks to a new ruling by the Forest Conservators, we are allowed to play six Sunday games on the Green.

- 18 November 1956 A sum of £1/1/0 donated from club funds towards the Hungarian Relief Fund.

- 6 January 1960 Offer received of £5 for the tent.

- 3 August 1960 Proposed and seconded that a propelling pencil be given to a young lad who helped clean the pavilion.

- 31 August 1960 The question of moving the bus stop was raised as there was a danger of those waiting being hit by the ball.

In 1958, Stan Croxon, who had been Woodford Green's scorer since the war, compiled a comprehensive record of averages and outstanding scores and partnerships (1947–1958 inclusive). This is a meticulous piece of work, showing that every single innings was timed to the minute. The figures are very revealing with regard to players and the improvements being made in the batting. They also contain incidental information which is interesting – for example, in the last game of the 1958 season Sid Springett of R.A.F.A.R.N.O. took all ten wickets on the Green in a sustained spell of bowling (10 for 28 in 25 overs, with 11 maidens) – the only time this had been recorded against the club.

From the mass of statistics assembled by Stan it is, perhaps, worth abstracting a few facts about Woodford Green C.C. in the post-war decade, 1947 to 1958:

A Woodford Green XI of the 1950s umpired by Mr Joe Root, one of the last farmers of Woodford.

FIRST XI

Played 233	Won 139	Lost 65	Drawn 16	Abandoned 13

SECOND XI

Played 182	Won 49	Lost 113	Drawn 11	Abandoned 9

SUNDAY XI

Played 199	Won 86	Lost 68	Drawn 34	Abandoned 11

The success rate of the 1st XI in this period was 59.66 per cent, with the most successful year being 1955 when sixteen of twenty matches were won. It is evident that scores were steadily improving in relation to earlier years, with the club scoring over 200 on several occasions and centuries and half-centuries featuring as never before. Six hat-tricks are recorded, and in one season A. Spicer took 147 wickets (1950). Although the club's playing strength numbered a regular forty, the statistics show that over 140 played for the Green during this period – though many played less than half a dozen games.

It is revealing, and indicative of village club cricket, to contrast the batting and bowling figures at this time, because the bowling averages are so much more impressive. The evidence suggests that runs were still hard to come by. Most of the players are very much still with us and they may be interested to be reminded of what they achieved. The following batting averages are for players who played over 150 innings between 1947 and 1958:

Player	*Inngs*	*Runs*	*Avge*
Barber	152	1562	11.57
Bird, Jas.	182	1389	8.85
Croxon	163	1008	7.25
Edwards	249	2561	11.04
Janes	209	3625	20.71
Menote	300	2255	8.32
Neat	182	2133	13.42
Powter	172	1415	8.80
Sheppard	278	3309	12.77
Wood, G.	177	2680	16.34
Woodroffe	200	1485	8.48

Two other batsmen are worth highlighting, although they did not play throughout the period and therefore played fewer than 150 innings. A. Spicer (1949–53) scored 2057 at 20.16 in 112 innings, and Stan Richardson (1953 on) scored 2967 at 24.72 in 141 innings. These are very high averages for the time, and both players continued to produce exceptional figures in the next decade.

The bowling figures are limited to those who took over 100 wickets:

Player	*Overs*	*Mdns*	*Runs*	*Wkts*	*Avge*
Beresford, R.	947.0	231	2453	221	11.10
Bird, Jas.	1853.3	487	4503	417	10.80
Budd	792.5	222	1749	158	11.06
Carter	595.2	174	1358	170	7.99
Chumbley	739.2	192	1807	151	11.97
Croxon	627.2	147	1549	182	8.51
Edwards	1596.0	287	4276	412	10.38
Figes	400.5	71	1056	100	10.56
Groves, Ron	368.5	120	638	120	5.31
Johnstone	1114.5	290	2811	314	8.95
Richardson	1618.4	302	4494	448	10.03
Smith, J.	487.1	109	1301	120	10.84
Spicer	1365.4	372	2849	417	6.83
Swingler	998.2	257	2397	314	7.63

The next generation produced an increasingly competitive side with some outstanding players. The club became a serious challenge to good opposition during the 1960s. For a long period in the sixties and early seventies Woodford Green had a very well balanced side, led by the excellence of Malcolm Bottomely as a batsman, John Chumley as a fast bowler and Geoff Wood as a wicketkeeper the like of whom nobody has seen since. These players were very ably supported by a loyal team of quality players who included Stan Richardson, Mike Curry, John Smith-Pryor, and Alan Sheppard. It is some indication of how good this side was to note that John Chumley was later to represent Leicestershire and that both he and Malcolm Bottomley are still representing their County Over-Fifties sides. They actually play against each other these days, for Hampshire and Essex respectively.

An overview of the club's progress in the later part of the century reveals steady developments in four areas. Firstly the dominance of batting over bowling reflects the vastly improved state of the grounds played on, including the Green. Secondly, the club's playing strength has been enhanced by a large influx of players whose background is the Asian Sub-Continent. Thirdly, the move to League cricket has sharpened concentration, both in the taking of quick singles and in fielding generally. Lastly, our Colts section has grown in five years to over a hundred young players who will hopefully secure the future of the club.

Again, club statistics and averages reveal a marked change in the balance of play during the later part of the century, with batsmen benefiting from better pitches. Between 1980 and 1999 a thousand runs were scored by players in a season 28 times, in contrast to the previous twenty years when only two players recorded this achievement. In 1990 three batsmen scored a thousand in the one season – D. Schofield, S. Newton and M. Bacchus. The most prolific batsmen in recent times, scoring over a thousand runs in a season, have been Steve Newton (9 times) and Alva Malcolm (8 times). Alva also achieved the double (a thousand runs and a hundred wickets) in 1982. The bowlers have had to work very hard to record good figures over the last twenty years - the top bowlers averaging 14 runs per wicket. The best returns have been those of Richard Dodson in 1983 (16–4–49–9) and Danny Graham in 1984 (7–1–23–10). The club's move to League cricket is recorded in a later chapter, and the future looks very promising with the development of a strong Colts section and the club being able, at the end of the century, to put out 3 Saturday and 3 Sunday teams

A.G.L./B.N.

Woodford Green team photos – top, from the late fifties; bottom, in 1983.

Three Local Heroes

Above: Steve Newton, a prolific batsman in the 1980s and 1990s, now holds the record score on the Green. 180 not out, against Roding Valley in 1994.

Left: Stan Richardson retiring from the Green. Stan was always among the top of the bowling and batting averages in the 1950s and 1960s. His score of 173 not out, made in 1959, was the club record on the Green for 35 years.

Dave Rowlands, who suffered two heart attacks while playing for the club, and continues to score runs after a heart transplant operation. Here he is hitting a six on the Green.

THE BARMAN'S TALE

The year was 1985 – the 250th anniversary of the club. It was decided to mark the event by selling beer at 1735 prices. Not surprisingly business was brisk. One member was overheard to say after his fourteenth pint: 'No more for me, I've spent fourpence already'. Mystifyingly, one of the more parsimonious members had not partaken of a single drink all morning and afternoon. When I asked him what was the matter he replied, 'I'm waiting for the Happy Hour!'

It is not easy to obtain a position as barman at the club as so many members are eager to do the job. Thus the club has been in the luxurious position of being able to pick only the best. It is not unusual after a game for players to rush off the field and shower and change quickly in order to be first there. In fact some players have been known deliberately to get themselves out early so that they can start serving before the game is finished. Such is the competition for the position of club barman.

Characters over the years have included a W.G. Grace impersonator who firmly argues that the club has never sold a decent pint of bitter. Another is a famed lion killer who takes an age to order a round. He asks for one drink and then disappears. Returning, he will ask for something else and disappear again. He will pay only when his entire table has been served individually. His record for buying a round stands presently at forty-seven minutes (12 October 1987). Another favourite of mine is a deranged dentist who claims that 'times are hard' before downing six pints and then going out to bat.

One will notice many strange bottles on the back shelf of the bar. This is generally due to the fact that someone has been on holiday to a distant land, tasted the exotic pineapple brandy (or whatever) and insisted that the bar chairman buy a bottle. The record for longevity is held by a bottle of 'Kuala' – a kind of chocolate whisky – which has been on the shelf, with one nip out of it, since the early eighties.

The record take for one day as shown on the till print-out stands at £130,097. This was achieved by my ringing in 130 (when bitter was £1.30 a pint), then sneezing and inadvertently adding three noughts. At £130,000 a pint we are approaching *Castle* prices!

The Wonders of Technology

Over the years modern technology has improved the lot of the overworked barman. Not least of these modern wonders is the automatic glass-washing machine, which is a treasure. It works like this:

1. Collect all glasses that are filthy dirty and covered in lipstick (the women's glasses are no better).

2 Place these in a tray and enter same into the *Super Duper Automatic Glass-Washing Machine*, and turn on. Wait for ten minutes.

3 Hey presto! Take out glasses. These you will find steaming hot, filthy dirty and covered in lipstick.

4 Wash them by hand.

Other devices include a fridge (which is currently preserving half a lemon, eight months old); a freezer – the door of which won't shut because no-one has defrosted it for five years; a knife for cutting lemons which has no blade; and a beer mug for the holding of biros (for the convenience of members) which has yet to contain a biro that actually writes.

Recognising the importance of the bar to the finances of the club and in order to bring it to state-of-the-art standard, bar staff have worked tirelessly and achieved national recognition. Awards won so far include:

1938 All Woodford Cleanest Spitoon Trophy.

1994 Best Kept Small Cellar (when the judges were inadvertently shown the Umpire's room).

1992 United Kingdom Best Potato Crisp Display.

1999 British Allcomers Oldest Bottle on the Shelf Cup.

May the good work continue. And now, drink up, please. The bar is closing. Cheers.

COLIN ROBERTS

6

League and Colts' Cricket

IN THE EARLY 1980s members of Woodford Green Cricket Club were reluctant to engage in League cricket, which was believed to be too competitive and aggressive and more suited to bigger clubs. Members preferred to continue playing village cricket. However, progressively, we found it more and more difficult maintaining the quality of fixtures we had been used to as the clubs around us were all joining leagues. The alternative was to resort to playing on public park pitches, which did not appeal.

Towards the end of 1986 we received a second approach to join the Essex Invitation League, an invitation having been declined when the League was first proposed in 1984. Following a referendum of the playing members a special meeting was called and an overwhelming majority voted in favour of our joining.

The application was duly made, but it transpired that the existing member clubs were not prepared to enlarge the single division and an insufficient number of suitable applications had been received to facilitate the creation of a second division. Our application thus remained pending.

However, in 1986, the club was invited to participate in the Lea Valley Mercury Cup, which involved our Saturday 1st XI in a limited number of games. Our Saturday 1st XI duly won the Championship in 1987 and were joint winners in 1988. Thus League cricket was introduced to the club.

We were eventually accepted into the Essex Invitation League in 1989 (now known as the Chargecrest Security Invitation League) together with Stanford-Le-Hope and Ongar. The membership consisted of Basildon, Billericay, Brookweald, Grays, Havering-Atte-Bower, Hornchurch, Snaresbrook, Theydon Bois, Old Westcliffians and Pegasus. The League programme involved both our Saturday 1st and 2nd XIs. Having accepted that we should play League cricket, we needed to tighten our organisation, bearing in mind that the league necessarily operated with strict rules and incorporated monetary fines for certain transgressions.

The League involved playing 45 overs per side with a limit of 12 overs per bowler. Both sides did pretty well in their first year and it was particularly gratifying that Derek Gardiner and his 2nd XI won the League 2nd XI Sportsmanship Trophy (based on marks awarded by the opposition during the season). The League also boasted a Panel of Umpires who did valuable work without fuss and in a professional manner, which was the envy of every other League in Essex.

With the withdrawal of the Chargecrest Security's sponsorship in 1990, the League Committee found new sponsors in Glayva Whisky and the League was renamed the Glayva League for the two years of their support. By 1992 Woodford Green C.C. was fully committed to League cricket. The game was without doubt competitive and played aggressively, but in the main remained friendly. It was generally agreed that the League encouraged much more enthusiasm and commitment from players at all levels; nevertheless, there remain a few who felt then, and still do, that League cricket had taken away the fun side of the game!

In 1992 the Glayva League was assimilated into the Morrant Essex League to form Division 2 of that League. The top two sides would be promoted to Division 1, the bottom two sides being relegated. The Morrant League played 100-over games with the side batting first allowed to play 54 overs with no restriction on the overs permitted to a bowler. Our first season in the Morrant League was a fairly successful one. Both 1st and 2nd XIs (captained by Steve Newton and Ajit Jethwa respectively) finished third – by far our best League performance.

Pattabi, best batsman and bowler in the Morrant Essex Cricket League, 1995

1993 saw our Saturday 3rd XI playing in the newly formed Division 2 of the Morrant 3rd XI League. The first season was triumphant, the transition being made competitively and smoothly by the captain, Brian Perring. Finishing third in their division, they were promoted to Division 1 for the 1994 season.

The League structure for the 1st and 2nd XIs remained the same until 1994, when the Morrant League reverted back to Division 1 with the departure of 18 clubs to the Colour Assembly League to form Division 2 of that League. Our application was unfortunately rejected as we did not fulfil the criteria of having two Colts sides. The year also saw the migration of a number of umpires on our panel. Pattabi, who had joined us from India, won the bowling award.

The year 1995 was a triumphant one for the club. Our 1st XI, under the leadership of Mark Halford, convincingly won the League Championship by the formidable margin of 45 points, and did not lose a single game during the process – an achievement to be proud of! Our own ace player, Pattabi, was by far the best all-round player on view all season. His personal tally of 778 runs and 59 wickets won him both the batting and bowling League awards, which will stand as the League record for years to come. Bob Newman had the highest average for the same season.

The Second XI championship was a far closer and more exciting affair, with 5 teams within 6 points before the last weekend. The weather – showery, with heavy bursts of rain – played a part in the results. Woodford Green, Hornchurch Athletic and Havering were unable to obtain a result, but Snaresbrook and Ilford Catholic both had decisive victories – the latter edging home for the Championship by just one point. Our Second XI (captained by Ajit Jethwa) finished 3rd in the League – a mere 3 points below the winners. The 3rd XI (captained by Sid Addatia) finished in eighth position.

In 1995 the Essex Cricket Association was committed to introducing a structured system of league cricket within the county. A sub-committee was appointed for the purpose of building a pyramid structure for League Cricket. The aim was to improve the standard of play at all levels of club cricket and to improve club facilities and amenities. To achieve these aims they proposed that the C.A.L. Division be opened up to allow promotion and relegation to the League below, as from 1997. This was rejected. We continue to play under the Morrant League.

In 1998 our 2nd XI, under the captaincy of Richard Locke, finished second in the League; Jacob Khushi was the highest scorer in the League. In 1999 Dave Roberts won the Batsman Award for the 3rd XI. The club's aim, at the end of the century, is to join the Shepherd Neame League, which has taken over from the C.A.L.

AJIT JETHWA

Opposite page: the 1995 Morrant Trophy. Below: the modern ground.

THE COLT'S TALE

Playing in men's cricket teams, when you are only fourteen years old, either means you are a quality player destined for a great future in the game, or that the team that picks you is desperate. In my case it was the latter. Anyway, I seized the opportunity to play in Woodford Green's First XI on a Sunday last year when I was asked.

I have to say that this was the most memorable match of my life to date – and probably will be forever.

It was an away game (I'd better not name the opposition), and we were put in to bat. There were some top players in the batting order so I felt there was no danger of me actually having to bat. However, just as England have a good top order on paper and then collapses, so it was with us.

Our Captain, as confident in our top order as myself, had popped down to the pub with another of our players for a quick drink ('to check it out for later'). The two were down to bat at ten and eleven.

Unfortunately, wickets fell more quickly than either of us could have anticipated. So it was that I found myself batting against the fastest bowler I have ever faced. It was then I discovered that this really was men's cricket.

So I blocked. Delivery after delivery, it seemed to me. I lost two partners at the other end and then realised with horror that there was no-one else to come in to bat if another wicket should fall.

As I blocked for what seemed like an eternity I saw two white shapes appear on the horizon – our returning captain with his prize bowler in tow.

Almost immediately my partner's wicket fell and the captain came in to bat. Alas, he fell quickly in a blaze of glory. His drinking companion then staggered out towards the wicket.

It was very evident that he'd had one or fifteen too many. He asked for a guard and proceeded to make a mark on the crease with his bat. The mark became a serious dent as he bashed away, and by the time he'd finished there was a hole in the wicket of serious depth (we heard later that it would take two years to repair).

To my astonishment, his lack of co-ordination was clear to everybody but himself. He boldly stumbled a third of the way down the wicket to block each delivery.

The weak summer breeze must have got up more than I'd imagined for every time he tried to hit the ball he fell over. Amazingly, he played ball after ball like this for seven overs while the opposition got angrier and angrier.

I was dismissed soon after his arrival, possibly because of lack of talent on my part, but certainly in bafflement at what I was witnessing at the other end of the wicket.

Eventually he ran himself out and followed me back to the pavilion with cries of 'lion-killer', directed at the umpire, ringing in my ears.

WILLIAM RHYS JAMES

The Colts

A most dramatic development in the progress of the club has occurred during the last five years, in which time a Colts section has grown to over one hundred members. These young players are coached on a weekly basis throughout the Summer and Winter months. The advantage to the club and its future is clearly demonstrated in the profile of the present League 3rd XI which has a core of Colts players. In the 1999 season Colts have also played in both the League 1st and 2nd teams. Beginning in 1994 with a small number of players from the age of 9 to 15, the club has rapidly developed a clear structure of Colts' teams at the ages of Under-9, Under-11, Under-13 and Under-15. The club has every reason to be grateful to those committed members who put in the time to coach and organise the matches for these boys who constitute our future.

Woodford Colts – the Under-16 XI, 1999.

7

The Grounds and the Pavilion

THE CRICKET GROUND at Woodford known at one time as the 'Castle Green' and now as 'the Green' has escaped development, and there is no evidence of this land ever being enclosed for farming or market gardening as in the case of adjacent land to the East. Maybe the soil was so poor that enclosing and claiming this ground was no prize for any would-be landowner. The land has always been part of Epping Forest and the hedge along Broomhill Road, according to the Woodford Historical Society, is probably 500 years old and marks the ancient boundary of the Forest. Whatever reason may be suggested for the lack of cultivation, the land has proved a perfect site for the playing of cricket since the eighteenth century.

The Corporation of London took over ownership and management of Epping Forest in 1878 and the ground then occupied by the club was deemed 'Land set apart for the use of playing organised cricket by Woodford Green Cricket Club' – and our licence was subject to the layout and maintenance of the ground being undertaken by the club. It might be said that this definition of 'land set apart' has often been misunderstood over the years by footballers, golfers wishing to practice chipping onto the square, even horse riders. Such activity is, simply, illegal.

Still playing on its original ground, Woodford Green C.C. is one of three cricket clubs who are permitted to play on Forest land, the others being Buckhurst Hill (who have a pitch opposite the

Roebuck Hotel, used since the 1860s), and Epping Foresters, who have played on Bell Common at Epping since 1947.

Grazing of Commoners' cattle on Forest land has been allowed for many years and large numbers roamed the Woodford area up until the 1970s. Manure was in abundance, and, before the club raised fences to keep cattle off the ground, a weekly task was to clear the playing area of all 'cow pats'. This was a job for players armed with wheelbarrow and shovel and strong stomachs (see 'The Captain's Tale', on p. 16). Players who resent unlocking the sight-screens and removing posts and chains guarding the square these days don't know they're born. Perhaps the sight of cattle crossing the main roads of Woodford in their unhurried way may never be seen again, because in 1988 cattle were prevented from grazing in the forest as a consequence of the BSE crisis.

The cricket ground set in land isolated from the main area of Forest by shops of the old village and residential properties, with two major roads on its boundaries, is a welcome sight to those returning from the hullabaloo of the City. Broadmead Road is to the North and in the 1960s was widened into a dual carriageway, forming the final link and through-road to Woodford Bridge. To the West side is the High Road, an old carriageway to Epping and

Opposite page: the original avenue of poplars planted to form the eastern boundary in the Victorian era.

Right: the statue of Sir Winston Churchill, Patron of Woodford Green C.C., 1951–1965.

beyond. This major traffic highway is always busy and is a feature of playing on the Green. Buses have for long been a target for ambitious visiting batsmen, and players are regaled on a weekly basis by a constant chorus of 'How's that!' from car passengers. An avenue of poplar trees, first planted in the reign of Queen Victoria, forms the East boundary, and to the South is a grassy plain leading down to a statue of Sir Winston Churchill.

The Churchill statue was erected to commemorate his services to the Woodford constituency as its Member of Parliament. The statue was unveiled by Viscount Montgomery in 1959, at which time Churchill was the patron of Woodford Green Cricket Club. The avenue of trees forming our Eastern boundary was cut down and replaced in 1968–69 on a slightly different line to focus on Sir Winston's statue.

During the Second World War public air-raid shelters were built on the Green, on the corner of the cricket field opposite *The Castle*. They were used during air-raids from 1940 on by local people who were to experience the vibrations of bombs exploding on the Southern area of the Green. The Congregational Church

adjacent to the Green was hit by flying bombs in 1944, having received two direct hits within three days, killing three people and injuring twelve. The above photo shows the damaged church during an early post-war game.

In 1946 the air raid shelters were removed and the land levelled and seeded by order of the local authorities. The work was poorly carried out and *The Guardian* reported that 'Green Cricketers Deplore Damaged Outfield', stating that the club were finding it hard to get Wanstead and Woodford Council to repair the ground properly. The area in dispute was enclosed with temporary fencing extending to within a few feet of the cricket table, causing great inconvenience during the playing season.

The club is entirely responsible for the financial upkeep of the ground and pavilion. Unfortunately, with no records available before 1939, we have no idea of the work carried out or the costs involved during periods of recession and unemployment. Since 1946 improvements have been continuous, and the ground at its best is an incomparable improvement on that of years ago when public footpaths criss-crossed the playing area.

Maintenance of the ground has always been a priority. We know that in 1886 a request was received by the Woodford Local Board for the use of their heavy roller on the cricket field. A letter sent by Woodford Green Cricket Club and signed by Mr Jessop was read to the Board meeting of 9 April, and the use of this roller twice a season was acceded to. Also, in a published financial statement for 1890, a high item of expenditure was for money spent on the ground – £7/15/8d.

The ground was maintained to an extent during the Second World War (1939–45). At the first post-war Annual General Meeting reference was made to two members present, George Gilbey and Frank Petherick, 'who when the younger members were away in the armed forces did in fact save the club'. They looked after the pitch and equipment, together with a small group of older club members with Jack Chumbley acting as holding Chairman. Cricket was played on the Green irregularly by members of the local Home Guard and A.R.P.

In 1946 the first attempt to level the unsightly and dangerous paths across the Green was carried out by a group of ex-servicemen, but with limited success. By 1951 the paths had widened and deepened and the top soil had been worn down to gravel, which made fielding a very hazardous procedure anywhere

near them. However, in that year work in digging-out, levelling and reseeding was successfully carried out by contractors. An appeal for the required £300 met with outstanding success, the money coming from club members and local shopkeepers, and the balance from club funds.

A major upheaval occurred to the ground in 1964 when the outfield and table had to be moved 65 feet to the South to enable the second carriageway of Broadmead Road to be built. Previously the road in front of The Terrace was a continuation of Broomhill Road and Horn Lane, only used by local traffic. The chestnut trees now on the grassed island in front of The Terrace used to form the Northern boundary of the cricket pitch. An old May tree and bush at the South of the ground had been a shelter and play area for children for decades. These were cleared and the ground levelled and drained by the local authorities at their expense under the supervision of a surveyor employed by the club.

Opposite page: The Terrace and the northern boundary of the Green in 1921.
Above: the Green, showing the High Road and the new boundary fence erected to keep out cattle.

At the same time as the dual carriageway was installed, a horse ride adjacent to the avenue of trees on the Eastern boundary became defunct, as the increased traffic on Broadmead Road made crossing very dangerous for riders and horses. With the permission of the Conservators of the Forest, the club was allowed to extend the ground over the area of the horse ride.

As well as the difficulties posed by the paths crossing the Green, the club had always experienced problems with the state of the outfield, which was never the finest in the district. By 1970 the outfield had deteriorated so much that no player felt safe when fielding and our opponents were hesitant to renew fixtures. Another major operation was undertaken, and in 1973 the outfield was ploughed, levelled and reseeded, leaving the square as an

> **Stone clearing operation helps pitch improvements**
>
> *Woodford Green Cricket Club are preparing for the new season by spending £500 on their pitch. The pitch is being renovated, levelled and re-seeded and work should be completed by the beginning of May.*
>
> *Sunday vice-captain and club press secretary Mr Clive de Boer said "We're hoping that the improved condition of the pitch will encourage more clubs to play on our High Road ground. Something had to be done because the outfield was too bumpy and uneven."*
>
> *Thirty sacks of stones were taken away from the pitch in a mass clearing operation on Sunday and Mr de Boer says that plans are afoot for the extension of the club pavilion. Members want a larger shed for cutting equipment and extra recreation space.*
>
> *Formed in 1735, Woodford Green are the second oldest cricket club in the country, and easily the oldest local club.*
>
> *● Our picture shows Woodford Green players and officials stone-picking on the new outfield surface. Left to right: Clive de Boer, Phil Hasler, Jacqueline Lindfield, Arthur Lindfield, Mike Kingswell, Bill Dodd, Bob Palmer, Richard Dodson and Geoff Wood.*

oasis of green in the centre of the ground. Because of adverse weather conditions and the acidity of the soil the ground did not recover in time for the 1974 season, and we could not host any other team on the Green in that year. However, in order to keep our tradition and record of unbroken play on the Green, one game was arranged at the end of September. Happily, the work eventually transformed the outfield to the flat grassed area that we have today. When the ground was scarified in order to remove the spreading thatch in 1997, and then reseeded again, the cost was £1,500 – three times the amount paid in 1973.

The standard of the ground at the end of the century is a tribute to the groundsmen and all the club members who have worked continuously to produce the playing surfaces now enjoyed by the club. The amount of time and care needed to carry out this work on a weekly basis is often overlooked. The club is aware of the commitment shown by these members and is forever thankful.

The Second Grounds

With the build up in membership by the early 1980s it was decided to form a 3rd XI. The requirement then was for a second

ground within a reasonable distance from the main ground and clubhouse. This did not prove easy, and so the first years were spent travelling to some distant 'home' grounds. Fixtures were arranged for a Saturday 3rd XI initially, but after two seasons a Sunday 3rd XI was also established. Since then the club has ambitiously put out six teams each weekend. The 3rds have played on a variety of pitches.

Firstly, between 1982 and 1983 Low Hall Farm, Walthamstow, was used. This ground gave us the longest distance to travel of any of our second grounds, with a grim access via the civil amenity tips. The team were followed by a service back-up group of two tea ladies, who set up teas in keeping with our club standard on tables provided in an old timber pavilion. The ground was maintained by Waltham Forest Council to a good standard, with a very good wicket. Unfortunately, on a cold day there was no escaping the vicious wind that reached us from a vast unsheltered area.

Between 1984 and 1986 we used Bancroft's Rugby Club ground, Buckhurst Way, Buckhurst Hill – ten minutes from the Green. We undertook all the work on an old cricket table laid out between

Rugby pitches. Teas and drinks were provided by the bar management. We were made most welcome until Bancrofts R.F.C. needed extra space for their pitches and the cricket table had to go.

Then between 1988-89 we had use of the Old Chigwellians Club, Roding Lane, a fine ground at Chigwell with a first-class pavilion. Our groundsman brought an old wicket up to scratch and we provided sight screens. Many enjoyable games were played on this ground.

In 1990 we were hosted by the Douglas Eyres Centre and Wadham Lodge – both grounds maintained by Waltham Forest Council. Douglas Eyres was renamed 'Goose Green' – not in respect of the Falklands War, but in appreciation of the mess left by a flock of geese which determined to a large extent where players actually fielded. Dressing rooms were 'top security', with locks everywhere, and the place was generally pretty grim.

In 1991 we moved to Nursery Road, Loughton, which was a lifeline allowed us by the Superintendent and Conservators of Epping Forest as this was part of the Forest 'set aside' for sport. Again, the club had to work hard to make a football area suitable for cricket, and as the ground had no amenities we had to hire a container to change in and a chemical closet (granted by Town and Country Planning!) Our intention was to install a small pavilion, but the costs involved of bringing water and electricity into service were prohibitive.

That brings us to 1992 and the sportsfield of Woodford County High School for Girls on the High Road, directly opposite our pavilion on the Green, where our 3rd XIs have played ever since. The ground is surrounded by trees with grass banks on three sides

---

Opposite: aerial view of the Green today, showing the Girls' High School and a glimpse of the club's second ground.

and is a perfect setting for cricket. A good deal of work had to be done to develop a square, but the club has made a firm commitment to maintaining the ground and the school has been very accommodating, for which we are most grateful. We developed two strips each year at a considerable financial investment. The club has settled in very happily to this idyllic setting and hope to play cricket on the ground for many years to come.

The Pavilion

In 1959 the first pavilion was constructed on the Green amidst much excitement. Rare permission was granted to build on Forest land by the Epping Forest Conservators.

For long before this, and up until 1956, firstly a tent and then a small marquee had been used to change or adjust clothing. Photographs taken in the last century and up to the 1920s show a small tent with a flag above a pitched canopy. This was so small that we can only assume most players came to cricket already changed. A small marquee was in use from the 1930s until the 1950s. This marquee was of sufficient size to be divided in two by

Opposite page: idyllic surroundings at the 3rd XI ground, Nursery Road, in 1991.
Above: an idyllic 3rd XI tea.

a canvas wall, one half being used as a tea room and the other half as a dressing/changing area. The whole thing was brought over to the Green from *The Castle* on a coster-monger's barrow. Tea was brewed in a large urn and carried over from a member's home in The Terrace.

Erecting this marquee and dismantling it after a game, and then storing it in an old hay loft above *The Castle* garage, proved so much of a chore that when two rooms became available in a High Road premises the club hired them. Between 1956 and 1957 rooms in an unoccupied house next to *The Castle* garage were used, and after that an actual garage became our changing room. This was a very primitive arrangement, with the club's tractor having to be removed before each game, so that oil and grease covered large areas of the floor.

This embarrassing arrangement threatened our fixture list, so that a pavilion became an absolute priority. Early drawings and the hopeful prospect of permission being granted by the Conservators kept us in business. Meanwhile, in the late fifties, teas were served in the open from a bench table positioned under the trees opposite The Terrace.

Our first pavilion was opened on 18 July by the Lord Mayor of London, Sir Harold Gillett, during the presidency of Colonel Sir Stuart Mallinson. The opening ceremony was supported by a large number of celebrities from the world of sport.

The building (30 feet by 12 feet) was a timber construction, lined externally in cedar boards with a cedar shingle roof, all erected on a concrete base. The pavilion was built by the local company of Wallace and Wallace at a cost of just under £1,000. There were separate dressing rooms at either end and a central communal room, but no services in the form of water, electricity or sewage. The boiled tea urn still had to be manhandled from The Terrace and toilet facilities found in *The Castle*.

The first pavilion, 1959.

The pavilion has been extended three times. Firstly, in 1965, an extension to the existing building was officially opened – again by the Lord Mayor of London, Sir James Millar – during the presidency of Sir Stuart Mallinson. Building work was carried out by the Matthews Partnership Ltd. The enlarged pavilion incorporated a store for ground equipment but also, most importantly, services were introduced which provided for ladies' and men's lavatories and a shower. An electricity cable was run into the building which provided for lighting and water heating for the first time, so our dependence on *The Castle* and The Terrace came to an end.

In 1980 the front of the building was extended by 7 feet by Kelly Builders. The work was carried out unobtrusively, with no formal opening. However the extra space was very welcome, and within two years we were granted a liquor license allowing us to open the

bar, at which members can here be seen convivially gathered on a Sunday morning ('Hence! home, you idle creatures, get you home' – *Julius Caesar*).

The last, largest and most costly extension was carried out in 1991. This enlarged the pavilion to an overall 45 feet by 28 feet. The opening was carried out by the local celebrity, John Lever MBE, the fine Essex and England bowler, during the presidency of A.G. Lindfield

The interior of the pavilion was completely replanned, with all areas increased in size and rooms added for umpires and scorers. Two schemes were prepared in 1988 by Richard Carrington, MA, Dip. Arch. (Cantab), RIBA, ACIARB, and submitted to the Epping

Forest Conservators. Official consent from all authorities for the preferred scheme was granted in 1990. Building work was begun in February 1991 by D. J. Burnham Builders. The final cost of all work, including structure, flooring and decorating came in excess of £35,000, the largest sum of money the club had ever underwritten. By diligent housekeeping and the generosity of many members (recognised as 'Friends of the Green') this debt has been paid off.

A.G.L./B.N.

THE TREASURER'S TALE

It was a wet Sunday evening in February. The clubhouse had never been as quiet. There was a collective silence in response to the chairman's announcement – 'And now for the vacant position of Treasurer.'

Our previous treasurer was moving out of the district due to his retirement. Of all the committee posts this was the one everyone dreaded falling vacant. No one ever wanted this job, yet it was vital. The club couldn't function without a good treasurer – especially now that we had a bar. 'I'll stand,' I said quietly. A proposer and seconder were found and the voting was completed in lightning quick time. The job was mine.

Alan Sheppard, my predecessor, had done the job very well for twenty years. It was going to be a hard act to follow. Still, I was a statistician, and I did work closely with the accounting department at work. Surely it couldn't be that difficult, could it?

I'm sure as I left the clubhouse that evening to stroll home, in the dark, across the muddy Green, the rain was falling harder and the wind was colder – or was it my imagination? Of course, as all club treasurers probably agree, it's not the budgets, accounts, bank reconciliations or invoices that are the problem. They are the easy bit.

The problems are:

- The unintelligible scraps of paper that surface in the bar receipts or match fees that have been put there in exchange for some unknown sum by some unknown person who has, quite probably, legitimately outlaid such an amount on the club's behalf.
- The embarrassment of having to ask old friends for their subscriptions for the umpteenth time, only to be told, 'I gave you that months ago,' or 'Are you sure I haven't paid?' (To be fair, I was embarrassed myself once, when an April-dated cheque surfaced from the bottom of my wife's handbag in September! I have solved this problem – by convincing the committee that we needed a Membership Secretary to administer subscriptions.)
- The impossible task of reconciling match fees to the number of team members, when there are an assortment of adult members, colts and guests, all paying different rates, with several still owing from the previous week.
- Counting the bar-take in the office on a Monday morning without being found out by the boss. I solved that first by becoming my own boss, and then secondly by handing the job to the Bar Committee.
- The recriminations when the bar stock-take shows a drop in percentage profit.

But none of these really equal what I shall call 'The chain of responsibility'. A few examples illustrate what I mean.

- *The treasurer's responsible for the insurance, isn't he?*

  So when the clubhouse is broken into he's responsible, isn't he?

  So he must be responsible for the alarm system –

  So when there's a false alarm it's his fault!

- *The treasurer's responsible for the money, isn't he?*

  Toilet paper is bought with money, isn't it?

  We've run out of toilet paper –

  Ask the treasurer why we've run out!

- *The club survives on bar revenue, doesn't it?*

  The treasurer knows we'll be in trouble if bar revenue falls –

  We might not be able to open the bar tonight, there's no one to run it –

  Give the treasurer a call!

I'm sure you get the idea.

But enough of the job as it is now. I've done it for fourteen years so it can't be that bad really. What about the past? What did previous treasurers have to contend with? At least I've got computer technology to help – they didn't! The club has been going for centuries and we've only been computerised for fourteen years. (And by the way the software I use isn't Year 2000 compliant!)

The Past . . .

The earliest evidence of the club's finances are from *The Woodford Times* of 21 February 1890, and report the accounts for 1889 as follows:

Receipts

Members' Contributions	£ 6	13s	6d
Subscribers	£20	4s	6d
Balance in hand	£ 0	9s	7d
Total receipts	£27	7s	7d

Expenditure

Stationery	£ 3 18s 6d
Bats, balls, etc.	£ 9 12s 6d
Umpires, scorers, etc.	£ 4 18s 0d
Ground repairs	£ 7 15s 8d
Balance in hand	£ 1 3s 2d
Total expenditure	£27 7s 7d

There are a number of interesting facets to this set of club accounts.

First, from a purely accounting point of view, there are two different figures for 'balance in hand'. I assume this means that the opening balance was £0 9s 7d (or about 48p in today's money) and a profit of £0 13s 7d was made on the year, leading to a closing balance of £1 3s 2d

Secondly, umpires and scorers were paid as early as 1889. I am sure most players of the current generation believe this to be a recent innovation. Obviously it is not.

Thirdly, the cost of equipment in the form of bats and balls was greater than the cost of ground maintenance. As you will see later, this is certainly not true today.

It is not clear how, in these early days, the income was derived and quite what the difference was between 'members' contributions' and 'subscribers'. However, by 1907 it is known that there was an annual subscription of two shillings. The table below shows how this has increased over the years:

1907	£ 0 2s 0d
1919	£ 0 6s 0d
1947	£ 1 7s 6d
1967	£ 2 10s 0d
1977	£ 4.50
1999	£75.00

This very clearly illustrates the inflation of the more recent years – though the 200 per cent increase between 1907 and 1919 shows that this was not unique.

. . . The Present . . .

Inflation has, however, not been the only reason for the need to increase revenues. Running a cricket club today is very different. As people's lives have become busier, both at work and socially, the extent to which work can be carried out by volunteers has reduced dramatically.

As mentioned above, the cost of ground work on the Green was approximately £8 in 1889. In 1998 it was over £5,000, and that does not include the capital cost of the many pieces of equipment needed to maintain the square and outfield to the standard now expected by players. Furthermore, we now have a second ground to maintain, for the 3rd XI. Expenditure on playing gear, in contrast, increased rather less dramatically – from £10 in 1889 to £580 today.

Even a relatively small club like ours now has the turnover of a small business, and all the administration that goes with it.

. . . and the Future

The costs of running the club will continue to rise faster than inflation. The trend towards less voluntary work and demands for better playing conditions will continue, and Inevitably this will put pressure on the finances. But I am confident that, as in the past, future treasurers will emerge from our 100-plus young members, with the ability to guide the club successfully through the next century and more.

They should, however, take note that my photograph used in the heading was taken around the time I began as treasurer. A more recent one showing the wear and tear might put them off.

RICHARD DODSON

8

Special Occasions

THE SOCIAL ACTIVITIES of Woodford Green Cricket Club have always been a major feature of its profile. The club has survived because of a very strong club spirit, often family-based, which has through the years never let slip an opportunity to celebrate whenever possible. We have already mentioned the great enthusiasm shown from the earliest days for the Annual General Meetings and the Annual Dinners, which were to become Dinner/ Dances. These are occasions when the club can celebrate its achievements and give expressions of gratitude to the officers who

Prizewinners at an Annual Dinner/Dance in the early 1980s with guest of honour John Lever, of Essex and England.

Toasts

"The King"

Hon. Secretary's Report.
Hon. Treasurer's Report.
Hon. Match Secretary's Report.
Presentation of Bat.

"The Woodford Green Cricket Club."
E. E. STARKE, Esq.

Reply to "The Club."
Mr. S. L. GREGORY.

"President, Vice-Presidents and Honorary Members."
Mr. G. GILBEY.

Replies to "Presidents, Vice-Presidents and Honorary Members."
A. E. CUTFORTH, Esq., C.B.E.
and H. J. BECK, Esq.

"The Visitors."

Replies to "The Visitors."
H. BOATMAN, Esq. and R. STEELE, Esq.

Artistes :

Mr. PETER KENNEDY
Bass.

Miss EMILIE F. GILPIN
IN
Comedy Character Songs and Studies.

Miss VIOLET SMITH
Solo Dance.

Dancing.

GOD SAVE THE KING.

NOTE.—A Motor Coach will leave for Woodford Green and South Woodford at (approx.) 11.45.

have seen the club safely through another season. From the beginning, awards have been given to the players who have been most impressive or who have shown the most marked improvement. The composition of a typical Annual Dinner in the early days is reflected in the bill of fare for the 1928 dinner, held at the Roebuck Hotel, as reproduced above.

These annual events are very much in-house activities, focusing on the club members. Other activities have brought the club to the wider notice of the community close to the Green, and have raised funds for either the club or for charity.

'The Green' has witnessed some grand occasions over the years. Mention has already been made of the spectacular Woodford Cycle Meet which was hugely popular in Victorian times. In 1946 the great victory celebrations attracted many thousands of people to a Gala day on Saturday 1 June. This was the climax of a programme of events over four days. The whole of the Green was taken over as a pleasure ground for young and old, with a variety of shows, band concerts, fireworks and a grand parade. A bandstand was erected opposite Chingford Lane and from this the Rt. Hon. Winston Churchill addressed the crowd. No cricket was played, but the victory celebration is recorded in the fixture card for that year – which also shows only one team playing immediately after the war, because many members were still awaiting demobilisation.

With the Compliments of

WOODFORD GREEN C.C.

President: SIR JAMES HAWKEY, BT.

FIXTURES, 1946.

Date	Venue	Opponent	Commence	Runs For	Against	Result.
May 18	H	Orford Baptists	2.30			
„ 25	H	Old Heronians	2.30			
„ 26	A	L.P.T.B.	11.30			
June 1		**Woodford Victory Celebrations.**				
„ 8	H	Hornchurch	2.30			
„ 10	A	Hornchurch	11.00			
„ 15	H	Imperial	2.30			
„ 22	A	Mann, Crossman	2.30			
„ 29	H	Craven	2.30			
July 6	H	Old Heronians	2.30			
„ 13	A	Imperial	2.30			
„ 20	H	Chadwell Heath	2.30			
„ 27	H	Waldon Sports	2.30			
Aug. 3	H	Craven	2.30			
„ 5	A	Mansfield	11.30			
„ 10	H	Hornchurch	2.30			
„ 17						
„ 24	H	Waldon Sports	2.30			
„ 31	H	Trenford	2.30			
Sept. 7						
„ 14	H	Chadwell Heath				

C. H. REASON, *Hon. Match Sec.*

The Woodford Green Cricket Club finds itself very heavily committed in this first Post War Season. Any help, however small, will be thankfully acknowledged by

Hon. Treasurer :
C. H. SANSON,
5, Eagle Terrace,
Woodford Green

Hon. Gen. Secretary :
H. HANCOCK,
51, Ingatestone Road,
Woodford Green.

To mark the Golden Jubilee of the Woodford Green Athletic Club and also to mark the granting of permission by the Epping Forest Conservators for us to build a pavilion, a double celebration took place on the Green in July 1958. Cricketers from both clubs, dressed in old-time garb, played a cricket match. This was preceded by a parade of brightly coloured veteran cars, the oldest being an 1899 Benz, followed by horsemen and horsewomen dressed in Edwardian costume. An old time musical show entertained a large crowd when the cricket match finished.

Two Fetes were organised by the club and held on the Green in 1977 and 1978. These were a rare concession from the Conservators of Epping Forest (our Landlords), granted because of the importance of the dates and the local nature of the celebrations. The fetes helped to raise funds towards the latest extension to the pavilion and they were very successful in attracting large crowds to the Green. The Woodford Green Silver Jubilee Fete, 1977, had many side shows and stalls, refreshment tents and a real ale bar. The central attraction was an old English cricket match between the Cricketers public house and the Green, which raised funds in aid of the Jubilee Hospital (now, sadly, closed down and replaced by a block of flats). The home team is portrayed in the top photograph opposite, and the away team is quaffing ale below.

In 1978 Woodford Green held a Forest Centenary Fete, pictured above, as part of the celebrations of the Epping Forest Act (which granted the Forest as an area for the pleasure of the people). With the experience of the successful earlier fete to draw on, the club made this another splendid day. Six tug-o-war teams from local public houses and Woodford Rugby Club shared centre stage. Again there were a number of side-shows and stalls, and good support from the public allowed for a donation to be made to the Epping Forest Centenary Fund.

The Hawkey Hall was hired twice in the early seventies for Club Discos, which were open to the public as fund-raising exercises. On both occasions the hall was crowded to capacity. Also as a fund-raising event, the committee decided in 1990 to organise a Grand Quiz open to other clubs and local organisations. This filled the Hawkey Hall and was such a success that the event was repeated in the following year. Sponsored ten-mile walks raised much needed money in the 1980s – these proving a fun event for some and the longest pub-crawl ever known to others.

In recent years the extended pavilion has allowed for out-of-season activities to be held and enjoyed by a greater number of members. Club quizzes have become regular events during the Winter, with club members alternating as quizmaster. Casino and race nights have also taken place, as well as international food evenings. The Annual General Meeting is now held in the clubhouse.

Every season tends to be introduced and concluded with games that have a social bias. Early on we have records of matches between the Captain's XI and the Vice-Captain's XI. This was followed by a 'Marrieds' versus 'Bachelors' match. Later, the season began with a trial match – the 'Possibles' against the 'Probables' – a good way to renew old friendships and introduce new members to the club (though, no doubt, some players would be anxious to prove a point, early on). In 1965 a single-wicket competition was started and ran until 1976 – some years being cancelled because of rain. The winners generally proved to be the better all-round cricketers – as recorded on the Cup awarded:

1965	Stan Richardson
1966	John Smith-Pryor
1967	John Chumbley
1968	Malcolm Bottomley
1969	Bob Palmer
1975	Bob Newman
1976	John Lindfield

Old-time cricket match on the Green

When more members wished to be involved in this annual event the club altered the format and in 1979 started a six-a-side tournament, which was an all-day competition played on a knockout basis. It was always interesting to see which six provided themselves with the most magnificent feast during the day. This event continued until 1988, and in the following year an annual reunion cricket match was inaugurated between the club and ex-players, who are called the 'Evergreens'. These former players, many of whom have had to move away, are always pleased to return and their nostalgia has been captured by Derek North in his version of *Nellie Dean* which is always sung after the game:

We're an old team on the Green,
The Evergreens.
Where we used to hit and dream,
The Evergreens.

And the avenue of trees
Seem to whisper in the breeze
You're our favourite team –
We miss you
Evergreens,
The Evergreens!

The Coronation in 1953 was celebrated on the Green with a cricket match against a specially selected XI brought by Jack Leiper. Jack was a very impressive player for both Woodford Wells

and Essex, and he was to continue his valued association with Woodford Green Cricket Club by organising a team to play us on the last Sunday of the season. This team was always guaranteed to include one or two county players, who were backed up by a formidably talented group. The annual match was always a very happy social occasion.

In 1980 the club toured for the first time. The five-day tour involved matches against Hampshire teams of varying strengths – from top Hampshire League teams to small village elevens. The

Hampshire location was the choice of the W.G.C.C. captain Chris Bunney who was born and brought up in the county. The touring party were based in Southampton and included a large contingent of wives, girlfriends and children, who duly attended every match and taxed the local tea ladies to the limit. The success of this tour was to make touring a very popular annual event thereafter. In the second year the base was moved to Winchester, which was not only a delightful city but closer to most of the grounds which we played on. Each year more people joined the party and the

Opposite: the teams for the Jack Leiper match, 1980s Above: Chris Bunney, the first tour captain, keeping wicket. Below: the first touring team in Hampshire.

tour required fine organisation to keep everybody happy. In 1984 the tour was enhanced by a weekend in Sussex prior to visiting Winchester. After ten years the club decided on a change of venue, and between 1992 and 1994 toured in Cambridgeshire from a base in St Ives. This was not so popular with club members and so a return to Hampshire was agreed, and this remains our annual location. Among the most regular teams that we have played on tour are Burley, Sparsholt, the Royal Army Pay Corps, St Cross and Broughton.

The club began playing cricket matches on Boxing Day in 1981, and these matches became a feature of the club's Christmas celebrations. Our opposition for many years was Wanstead Cricket Club. This game was played in all weathers – winter sunshine, frost and even snow. The pitch markings on the snow-covered ground were carried out in creosote. Batsmen were sponsored for

Above: a Boxing Day team braves the elements.
Opposite page: cartoon memories of the club on tour.

ARTHUR LINDFIELD
'THE CHAIRMAN SPEAKS"

WANSTEAD & WOODFORD

REDBRIDGE

Guardian

AND

Independent

Week ending Friday, January 2, 1981 Vol. CX 5781 12p

England Test star cracks a 51 not out for chairity

SANTA at the stumps, and the oddest cricket match on Woodford Green since 1735 helped raise about £1,000 for Brookfield House School on Boxing Day.

Essex and England star bowler John Lever returned to the pavilion as top scorer after an unbeaten 51. But at bowling — he failed to take a wicket!

John's efforts were enough to send the Woodford Green Cricket Club to a 123 for nine victory over Wanstead Cricket Club's 116 for 10.

The charity match was the brainchild of Brookfield House Parent-Teacher Association chairman Bob Palmer. He hopes it will become an annual event.

Each player had to pay to play and more cash was raised from spectators and a raffle.

Top priority for the PTA's fund raising at present is a tail-lift mini-bus for Brookfield House, which is renowned as one of the foremost schools for the physically handicapped in the country.

The mini-bus will cost about £17,000. The PTA is also raising cash for special lifting wheelchairs, ordinary wheelchairs, wide-keyed calculators and other equipment which cannot be provided by the local authority, to help maintain the high educational standards and level of life at the special school.

Pint in hand, a laughing John Lever takes it easy as he waits to bat on Boxing Day. (204)

their runs and a large amount of money was raised for charity. The sight must have been amazing to passers-by, but the atmosphere in the pavilion was always tremendous with players and supporters well stimulated with hot punch. Perhaps it was the hot punch, perhaps the half-century which John Lever scored when he turned out for the club on Boxing Day 1981, but the local paper's headline, above, let a misprint through the covers.

Celebrations for the 250th Anniversary of the club took off with a grand Dinner/Dance at the Sir James Hawkey Hall on Friday 3 May 1985. This was followed in mid-Summer with a cricket week held on the Green. W.G.C.C. entertained Essex C.C., a 'World of Sport' XI, Harlow C.C., and a Jack Leiper XI. The final game was against an Old Woodford Green XI. Unfortunately the week's cricket was badly affected by poor weather, but the club was in vibrant form. The hosts for the first game against the Essex XI were the Epping Forest Committee of the Corporation of London, who arranged a luncheon served in a marquee on the Green for over sixty people. The table plan provided for the Mayor of Redbridge, three local M.P.s, dignitaries from Epping

Celebrities on the Green. From the 'World of Sport' XI in 1985. Former England fast bowler Fred Rumsey, New Zealand and Surrey Captain Geoff Howarth, and all-in wrestler Mick McManus – showing the right spirit!

Forest and the Corporation of London, Essex County Cricket Club, Buckhurst Hill and Epping Foresters C.C.s as well as the two teams, umpires and scorers. The year's celebrations ended with the annual Boxing Day match against Wanstead.

A first for the club was the Inaugural Colts Presentation Evening held on Saturday, 4th September, 1999. Awards were presented to the four age groups of our younger players: Under-9s, Under-11s, Under-13s, and Under-15s. The afternoon was taken up with a single wicket competition; later the presentations and the fun evening were well supported and a great success. A.G.L./B.N.

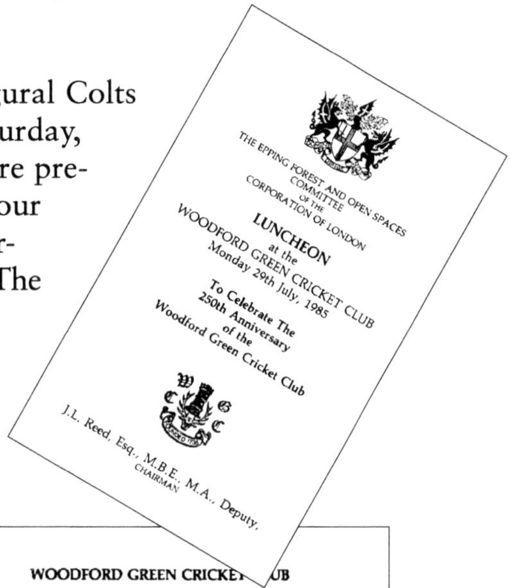

THE EPPING FOREST AND OPEN SPACES COMMITTEE OF THE CORPORATION OF LONDON

LUNCHEON

at the

WOODFORD GREEN CRICKET CLUB

Monday 29th July, 1985

To Celebrate The 250th Anniversary of the Woodford Green Cricket Club

J.L. Reed, Esq., M.B.E., M.A., Deputy,
CHAIRMAN

Menu

Ogen Melon with Grapes
Mouscadet de Serve et Maine

***

Fresh Poached Scotch Salmon
Garnished with Asparagus Tips
and served with a Dill Mayonnaise
Hot New Potatoes
Full Seasonal Mixed Salad
Château Rousselle 1978

***

Fresh Strawberries and Cream

or

Cheese Board

***

Coffee

Toasts

THE QUEEN

THE LORD MAYOR
THE CORPORATION OF LONDON
AND THE SHERIFFS
Proposed by: The Chairman

WOODFORD GREEN CRICKET CLUB
Proposed by: The Chairman

WOODFORD GREEN CRICKET CLUB

Woodford Green Cricket Club was founded in 1735. Although cricket was played long before 1735, there can be few cricket clubs surviving to-day that can celebrate a 250 year anniversary.

In the early days of cricket the bat resembled a crudgel of some 2½ inches in diameter at the bottom end, tapering towards the top, or handle, to form a convenient grip. It was about 3 feet long and the bottom part was slightly curved. The leather ball had not been invented and instead the players used a stout stick of some 4 inches in length. The batsman was known as the striker and his 'runs' were scored on a length of thick stick by notches being cut into the wood.

Since its foundation the Woodford Green Cricket Club has played on Epping Forest land alongside the High Road, Woodford Green. Originally the playing pitch was prepared by cutting the grass with a scythe, then watering it from pails carried from nearby ponds and finally levelling out with wooden rammers.

The 'Cattle and Two Brewers' coaching inn was used by the young club for its meetings and 'The Castle Hotel' which later replaced it, continued to be the Club's 'headquarters' (with one or two short intervals) until the pavilion was enlarged and services laid on in 1965. The pavilion was opened by the Lord Mayor, Sir Harold Gillett in 1959 and the extension by the Lord Mayor, Sir James Miller.

Today the Club has a total membership of 140 and fields 6 XI's, three on Saturdays and three on Sundays. It is a member of the Club Cricket Conference.

THE SPECTATOR'S TALE

Why Woodford Green – and why cricket?

I have asked myself this question many times over the years that I have been a supporter, most notably of the bar.

Unlike many who profess to know the game I don't really know it all. Of course, I can tell you the fielding positions (just), and what the umpire is signalling to the scorer ('Leave some sandwiches for me'), and the batsman's coded messages to his colleagues on the boundary ('My box is rubbing'), but when the game's finer points are discussed then I am lost.

I do not know my popty[1] from my pongo,[2] my sostenuto[3] from my spectacles.[4] And that, in part, is cricket's fascination. For you can watch two games of soccer, possibly played an ocean apart, and they may be almost identical in their patterns of play. One–nil to the Arsenal. One–nil to Boca Juniors. Yawn. Boring.

---

[1] Popty – a slow ball, bowled underhand, pitched just outside of the batsman's reach with a break to the off (a term now almost obsolete).

[2] Pongo – for a bowler to get hit around.

[3] Sostenuto – a ball that pitches on the leg and hits the off.

[4] Spectacles, pair of – a duck in each innings.

Cricket is not nearly so predictable (England batting collapses apart) and certainly isn't dull, no matter what its detractors may say. It is rare indeed to leave a cricket match without learning something, perhaps concerning a quirk in the laws, perhaps concerning a quirk in the umpires, but it's a fair bet that at every cricket match something *different* will happen.

Spectators may not be acquiring great technical knowledge of the game when they watch Woodford Green (just what *is* reverse swing?) but they will learn a fair bit about character, sportsmanship and common humanity when they spend a summer's afternoon with us.

So what have I learnt from my years with the club?

Well, quite a lot actually. In my very first season I found out how one tends to a bleeding player when the first-aid box is empty (use bog roll), how to make a telephone call from the bar without paying (there's a secret phone number), where to find the playing cards when Sheila, our former bar chairman, has hidden them (back cupboard, bottom shelf) and where to buy a good joint (at the local butcher, of course).

In the end I suppose the entire game comes down to character. And that is something which Woodford Green has in abundance.

Take, for example, Bobby Newman, the Saturday 1st XI captain – red-haired, freckle-faced, eternally youthful and enthusiastic. Now Bobby is a class player – overlooked by England, of course, but what a tonking he'd give that upstart Shoiab Akhtar if he'd been given the chance.

And Alva Malcolm, a tall, wiry, athletic Jamaican. A mere boy at 57 years of age. His best years still lie ahead. Sort out Alan Donald? He'd bat that so-called quickie out of existence if he set so much as a South African toenail on our pitch.

And while we're on the subject of elite players, it's very lucky for Shane Warne that he's playing for Hampshire in the year 2000. He clearly didn't relish facing Neil Day, who would flippin' murder 'im, to coin a phrase.

Oh yes.

In the Long Room at Lords they may talk of Compton, May and Edrich, of Hutton, Gooch and Bailey. But here in Woodford Green, in the cold dark hut which we call a pavilion, in this cosmopolitan but essentially very English corner of England, we talk of Lindfield and Richardson, of Naismith and Wolstenholme, of Baker and Beck, of Wood and Howe.

Forget professional cricket. Apart from anything else, there is also the prospect of the genuine, home-spun excitement of watching a thrilling finish on the Green. At our level sides go for a result. Those clubs that don't get 'the look' from Sheila Baker the next time they turn up. That teaches 'em.

I remember one favourite moment, an evening that glows gold in the mists of time and recollection. And this is that story . . .

There's a breathless hush on the Green tonight.
A bumping pitch and a blinding light,
An hour to play and the last man in . . .

A tall young man marks his thirty-pace run-up. He has been going through the Woodford batting like a dose of salts. A new batsman comes to the wicket and cuts the bowler for four. Next ball and the batsman tries the same shot. This time he's out – caught, I think.

This means that our last pair is at the wicket – but what a pair. Step forward 63-year-old Robin Wolstenholme and 50-something heart transplant recipient David Rowlands.

With an insouciance that would do credit to Raffles, Robin Wolstenholme rambles to the crease. Fast bowler champing at the bit, our man takes his guard and, more importantly, takes his time.

The opposition are chatting and laughing. Clearly, this white-haired old gent isn't going to pose too much of a problem. Wolstenholme looks at his most passive and genteel. At the other end, Dave Rowlands is smiling his ruddy, amiable smile. Deceivers both.

Wolstenholme straightens his bat as the bowler comes in. The two spectators – me and my Jack Russell – are anxiously pondering the outcome of such lively bowling against two batsmen who certainly have more of a cricket past than a cricket future.

The bowler bowls. Blocked. End of over. Dave Rowlands is now facing. He blocks. Since neither batsman has dreamt of taking a quick single since the 1960s there is no communication problem between them to worry about.

Wolstenholme faces again at the other end. He drops his bat on to the ball and blocks. Ball after ball. The other team is getting more aggressive in the field. The bowlers are getting even quicker. The truth has dawned. These two plan on saving the match.

There is nothing the opposition can do. They try everything, but Woodford Green claims the draw. A moral victory, at least. Funnily enough, I can't remember who the opposition were, but I well remember that autumn evening. When I am old I will recall how, suddenly, three dozen or so people appeared from nowhere to see the last few overs. And of Wolstenholme (now retired) and Rowlands (still playing as I write), at their most cussed, irritating best.

And I truly hope that my son, Rhys, will enjoy moments such as that in his playing and spectating life with Woodford Green. Character, that's what it's all about.

JILL JAMES

9

Evergreen Memories

On tour in 1984 we played Bexhill, a premier side in the Sussex League. The home side scored a formidable total, in excess of 250. It was not long before I was heading for the crease with our side struggling at 40 for 4. A skipper's innings was called for. I had a good partnership with Danny Graham (who had a three pound bat and a waist to match), and it was noticeable how the small stand was filling up with spectators. We lost more wickets, but kept chasing, and with the last man at the wicket we won in the last over. I was 127 not out. Bexhill took their defeat quite well, believing that they had lost to Woodford Wells, the Essex premier side. When they began to discover that in fact they had lost to Woodford Green, a village team nobody had heard of, humiliation began to sink in. It was just the opposite for us. BOB NEWMAN

Tony and I crossed to the Girl's School to see how the Thirds were getting on. It soon emerged that only one run was needed for them to win and at the wicket was one of our notoriously selfish batsmen (to be nameless, of course) – on 49. The last ball of the over was bowled at his partner, who let the wide ball go and the wicket-keeper missed it. 'Stay there!' said our man, declining the easy byes on offer and wanting his 50. He was now facing, and defended the first two balls. The third hit him on the pad as he played way forward. Tony, spectating from the boundary, yelled 'How is he!' and our umpire gave him out. BRIAN PERRING

When I was a boy, long before the war, I used to help the groundsman prepare the wicket and mark out the pitch. He would give me a penny which I spent either on 'stales' from the cake shop or 'specks' (bruised fruit) from the greengrocers. I'd spend the afternoon watching the cricket and eating the goods.

I remember when I was skipper on a Bank Holiday Monday we usually had an all-day game starting at 11.30. On one occasion we had a guest fixture against a coloured side. They batted all morning and all afternoon, and I was most upset when after tea they still decided to bat on, so I had words with the skipper. He said 'You bloody put us in. You bloody get us out!'

RICHARD (DICKIE) EDWARDS

Billy Rustall was umpiring for us in a Wells game when a formidable batsman called Greene was batting. The cricket was tense. When Greene was hit on the leg Rustall himself shouted 'Hout!' This was followed by a proper appeal from the bowler. As he passed Rustall on his way to the pavilion the batsman asked: 'Rustall, what do you mean by giving a man out when nobody has appealed?' 'Oh well, sir', replied Billy, 'you know yourself you *was* out, don't you, sir?'

BABS SANSOM

Annual dinner/dance at the Royal Forest Hotel in the late 1940s.

I remember in 1946, after the war, when we were trying to get the outfield going so that we could get a bit of practice one night, a chap came riding up on a bike and he says, 'Is this the Woodford Green Cricket Club?' and we said, 'Yes.' He said 'Oh, I'm the captain'. That was Stan Wright. We'd never seen him before. He'd been appointed by the Chumbley family who had kept things going during the war and were related to him. He started off as first team captain.

Nobody had any money in those days, and nobody had a car. I remember when we had our dinner/dance at the Royal Forest Hotel one year a gang of us missed the last bus home and we had to walk. At my suggestion we took a short-cut through the forest. Unfortunately we came across a lot of mud and puddles at night and all of our best suits and dresses were ruined. We got home quicker, but I wasn't overly popular.

LES POWTER

We were playing against Wanstead on one occasion and their regular fast bowler Neville was bowling his usual immaculate line and length. When I got to the crease Brian Perring advised me, as he did every time I played for him, 'Play yourself in and have a good look at it'. My first ball I pulled to mid wicket for four. The same went for the second. Perring was glaring at me. As I continued to hoick across the line Neville was getting increasingly wound up. The more I slogged the more distressed he got. After I pulled a ball off middle stump for 6 he yelled, 'That was a bloody awful shot!' I replied 'That's the best I can do with that type of bowling'. He went to pieces after that and was taken off. Perring was most amused. TONY RUDELHOFF

Caesar Hoy told a story that goes back to the nineteenth century when The Terrace, adjacent to the Green, was called Bailey's Row, at the end of which was a wooden structure owned by a carpenter called Mr Wood. He could not, or would not, pay the Queen's Tax, and so the authorities had the building pulled down, leaving him sitting in a chair under the stars. And there he sat for three days and three nights!

A certain umpire, in his anxiety to interrupt the game as little as possible, was not too meticulous in giving guard. One incoming batsman who had received what he thought to be covering middle and leg said: ' I say, are you sure that's all right?' To which came the umpire's reply: ' Hold your bat up straight and I'll give it to you properly!'` FRED KNIGHT

The year was 1989, the opponents were West Essex at their ground, the umpires were two Woodford stalwarts Ian Fullbrook and Ross Walker, and the bowler was John Bernard. The batsman played a full-blooded hook shot, which was unusual, as John was not getting much lift. Every eye, including the batsman's, switched to the leg side. I was fielding at slip when this red blur passed in front of me. I dived to my right and as my elbow hit the ground, the ball stuck in my hand. It was probably my best catch, of many, for the Green. But what made it memorable was the fact that the bowler apologised to the batsman as he walked off. Such is cricket! DON COATES

I once had the honour and privilege to be selected for a game against Cheshunt 3rd XI. *Charlie Chin, the captain, phoned me on the Monday and told me where to go. We all turned up at what was a magnificent ground and sports centre. Unfortunately it was drizzling, but the opposition could be seen in the pavilion, ready for the game. As we approached, we saw two teams coming out to play. 'Sorry', we were told, 'but you're playing over there' – and somebody pointed to the adjacent cow field. This is where our match took place, in the rain, with me and Arthur Lindfield umpiring and getting soaked. We lost several wickets before I was relieved and I joined Arthur in his car. I happened to ask Arthur, 'What number am I batting?' He got out and asked the scorer who was sitting in the next car. 'Sorry, Colin,' he said, 'It doesn't look as if you're playing.' Charlie, without knowing it, had brought twelve players. Perhaps Chinese adding-up is different to ours.*

COLIN ROBERTS

I was bowling to my usual field, set for catches from ambitious batsmen. Predictably I was miss-hit to deep mid-off. We all looked for the catch to be taken, but the carefully placed fielder (a sharp businessman) was seen to be talking on his mobile-phone. The catch went begging and I was livid. 'What's going on?' I asked. 'Sorry Robin,' came the reply, ' but I have just sold a Mercedes.'

ROBIN WOLSTENHOLME

Reg turned up to his first game for the Green dressed immaculately in lovely whites. This impressive figure was put in to bat early on. Very soon he received a ball from the Hornchurch Athletic bowler that beat him all ends up. It was caught by the wicketkeeper amidst cries of 'Howzat!' from all sides. The umpire deliberated and declared. 'Not out.' Reg then threw off his gloves and wrung his hands in a very public display of physical hurt. Hornchurch were not amused, we were embarrassed and so was the umpire. Reg couldn't understand the fuss. It turned out that this was indeed his first game and he didn't know you can be caught out off your gloves. A.G.L.

'On Woodford Green with Bat' used to be rendered very effectively by the Saturday 2nd XI *at the end of the day when they were well drunk. It uses the tune of 'On Ilkley Moor'.*

Where hast tha bin since I saw thee
On Woodford Green with bat
Where hast tha bin since I saw thee . . . *etc.*

How were thee out last time
On Woodford Green with bat . . .

I bin a caught in the slips,
On Woodford Green with bat . . .

How many runs did thee last score,
On Woodford Green with bat . . .

I got another golden duck,
On Woodford Green with bat . . .

Where hast tha bin since I saw thee
On Woodford Green with bat . . .

I bin a shovelling up the sh–t
On Woodford Green with bat . . .

ROBIN NORTH

I remember two outstanding results for us playing away against very strong opposition. At Saffron Walden we played with eight men and they scored 230. We got them for 4, with Bottomley and Howe putting on 150. At Stort we made a record score for their ground of 298 for 6 (Stan Richardson scored 98). I thought 'I'll never see this again.'

Ken Carpenter, a good batsman, was picked for 3 matches one Bank Holiday weekend – to bat at number 6. He went to Southend on the Saturday, the Wells on Sunday and to Stort on the Monday. He travelled half of East Anglia to play cricket and never got in. He didn't face one ball in three games.

JOHN ANDREWS

Archie 'Spot' Smith was a really big hitter. He had arms like Popeye. Regularly he would hit the ball over the trees and out of the ground. His response was always: 'Come, one.'
DEREK NORTH

There was only one thing to say to a protesting batsman, and I said it all the time: 'Look in the book!'
ANDY AUSTIN

What I remember most was the fixture list on Sundays, when we mostly played away, which was really marvellous. We played some excellent teams and our Sunday side was *the* team to play for.
STAN RICHARDSON

I remember bowling uphill against a young player at Tottenham (G.N.E.R.). The batsman got an outside edge and we all appealed. The umpire said 'Not out'. 'Thanks, Dad,' said the batsman.
JOHN LINDFIELD

For three years the Saturday 2nd XI used a nicely shaped chunk of wood – called the Crugby ball – for catching practice before a match. This treasure was later mounted and put on show in *The Castle* until a cleaning lady threw it away. After this we used a cricket ball for practice, but you could never be sure whether the object coming at you was the ball filled with lead, the lopsided ball, or the hollow one. D.N.

In the 1960s and 1970s wives and girl-friends accompanied their menfolk to away games more often than now. Whether this was to enjoy the day in the country, the cricket, or to ensure their prompt and sober return is a matter for conjecture. On some of these far-flung and often rurally situated fields the lavatorial arrangements were somewhat basic. At Henham, for instance, a gesture to the modesty of the ladies was afforded by a segment of Anderson shelter laid on end forming a U-shaped screen some three feet high behind which the fair sex could squat while maintaining a clear view of play. One of our more fastidious matrons, shocked at the lack of proper toilet paper, maintained that it was necessary to 'Shake it about a bit to dry!'

For one lady of nervous disposition, as well as acute arachnaphobia, Bayford and Hertford Nondescripts holds nightmarish memories. The 'domestic' arrangements at this ground at the time comprised a corrugated iron shed containing a chemical loo and whose door's propensity to swing open was checked by the agency of a piece of string clutched by the user. This structure was situated just outside the long leg boundary.

Our lady of nervous disposition (LND from now on), after having consumed a couple of drinks in the pub en route and a cup of tea or two from the Thermos flask of one of our more experienced matrons, finally succumbed to the urgent call of nature and, suppressing her fear of lurking spiders and beetles, made the necessary visit. Imagine, then, the scene on the long leg boundary: LND with door string clutched in one hand, skirts etc. fastidiously kept from the surrounding squalor in the other, poised uneasily one inch away from the seat, warily eyeing the larger arachnids and entomological specimens and surrounded by rust-flaked corrugated iron.

Out on the cricket field a Bayford and Hertford bowler lets slip a leg-side full toss to one of our best hookers, husband of our LND, who dispatches the ball directly towards the corrugated iron roof . . .

DAVID BAKER

The Silver Jubilee Fete (7 June 1977) was a very special day on the Green. It was also a triumph for the social committee who had spent months planning, begging, cajoling and bonding far and near. The Epping Forest Conservators had been very specific: 'Nothing goes up before sun-up, and everything must come down and be tidied away by sunset.' So we had to be very well organised. It was a grey, dismal dawn – appropriate 'Coronation' weather – but spirits were high as we decorated our stalls red, white and blue. Spirits grew higher as things fell into place: coloured stalls, our 'Bank on Wheels', tea-tent and real-ale bar, and all of us dressed to kill in period fashion. And then the public arrived in droves.

The lady on the flower stall started the shouting: 'Get your Lizzies here – they're not going anywhere unless you buy'; a stroppy youth who claimed he'd won on the 'Spin-the Wheel' was threatened with the stallholder's father; the real-ale seller made a bomb and tripped over his boots carrying an upturned dustbin lid full of cash to 'the bank' – a grin on his face as wide as the Thames Estuary.

At the Tombola stall an aged lady protested at winning an envelope marked 'Dinner for Two, and Wine (at a famous West-End restaurant)'. 'I'm too old for that,' she claimed. Whereupon my husband offered her £20, which she happily accepted, and a month later I was the happy recipient of the win, able to re-live a sunshine day, despite the clouds. ANNE WOLSTENHOLME

All the fun of the fair at the 1978 fete, which attracted a large crowd to the Green. Opposite page: tug-o'-war. Left: the lucky dip . . .

Our Saturday 2nd XI League match against Eton Manor (July 1995), played on the Green, was exceptional. We had built a reputation of scoring heavily during the season, achieving targets of over 200 runs on five occasions. On this day Eton Manor amassed a huge score of 297 in 49 overs (in a 100-overs game). At tea they were cock-a-hoop, and were certain they could not lose. Their confidence was boosted when we were quickly reduced to 11 for 2 in the seventh over. Then entered our star player of the season, Ghulam Fareed, who had already amassed 250 runs in the 5 games he had played to date. Fareed scored 68 at a blistering rate and took the score to 82 in 14 overs, putting us back on track. On his departure we lost 3 quick wickets and were 105 for 5 after 19

Not so evergreen, but still a vivid memory for many – damage after the great storm of 1987.

overs. In came Mohammad Abass who confidently added 105 runs in 13 overs with Riz Mohammed. Abass scored a scorching 79, taking us to 211 for 6 in 32 overs. Riz (29) and Steve Gage (22) then took over the challenge. In the 38th over we were 265 for 8, still needing 33 runs. Paresh Patel (26 not out) and Terry Ereira (10 not out) scored the winning runs in the 44th over with 7 overs and 2 wickets to spare. History was made – we achieved the highest score by the side batting second on the Green.

AJIT JETHWA

THE UMPIRE'S TALE

It is a glorious hot day and the Green are playing a friendly Sunday match. Starting time approaches and the home team are busy with their preparation – consuming as many pints as possible before cricket interrupts the main proceedings of the day. Opposition members join them in the bar as they arrive. Meanwhile the home captain is carrying out all the pre-match duties on his own – unlocking the sight-screens, putting out the boundary rope, removing the shutters, etc.

The captains toss and the Green are in the field. As usual the opposition have no umpire (arguably a fortunate detail given the size of the umpire's room), so I sort out a coat, bails and six stones. I try to explain to their captain the complicated local rules regarding the fences, trees and boundaries around the Green but he is much more interested in his pint.

A player is eventually forced to umpire with me and we all stroll onto the field only twenty minutes late. I glance at the clock, which miraculously shows the time to be two o'clock – well, never mind. I am properly dressed for umpiring, wearing dark trousers, a white coat, clean shirt and tie. The player umpire ventures out with a cigarette in his mouth, wearing the unbuttoned umpire's coat over a pair of shorts – and that is all he's wearing!

As we are about to start I exchange the match ball for the bowler's cap, designer sunglasses and asthma puffer. As an afterthought the wicketkeeper asks me to hold his cigarettes and matches and spare contact lens. Considering that that my pockets are already filled with a spare ball, bail and

counter – not to mention six stones, a bar towel, a penknife, nail clippers and sticking-plasters – I am struggling for space.

As the match gets under way I notice that the player umpire has now finished his cigarette but has produced a pint from one of his pockets and a packet of crisps from the other. He is enjoying a private picnic at square leg!

The match continues until the peace of the afternoon is shattered by a loud and confident appeal from wicket-keeper and close fielders for a stumping. We all look to square leg where the umpire is concentrating his attention on the legs of a young girl walking past the boundary. The appeal goes unanswered.

By now the sun has attracted quite a crowd, who encroach onto the field of play to avoid the shade. However, in a spirit of goodwill the players and I ignore this intrusion. We also ignore the regular cries of 'Owzat!' from cars passing along the High Road. Whatever happened to imagination?

Eventually I am called into action when one of the away batsmen gets a thick edge and both wicket-keeper and slip appeal loudly. He is clearly and obviously out, but makes no effort to acknowledge the fact. I give him plenty of time to walk – or am I just torturing him? Finally I have no option but to raise the dreaded finger. He reluctantly leaves the field after giving me the evil eye. So much for friendly cricket!

After various changes of player umpire in miscellaneous forms of dress, the first innings is eventually over and the highlight of my day arrives – tea! I eat as many sandwiches and cakes as I can in the time available, and in a loud voice begrudgingly inform the home batsmen that there are five minutes left before the restart. This information is really intended to alert the opposition, who are nowhere near finishing their tea, that a cricket match is being played. However, as usual, it is a waste of breath and I find myself standing at the wicket, all alone and ignored by the players, for quite some time.

When the Green do start batting they lose a wicket in the first over. We wait for the number three, and we wait and we wait. Eventually out strolls one of the Green's top batsmen (rumoured to have killed lions – which might be true, because none have been seen on the Green recently). The bowling is fast and furious but the ball keeps disappearing to all corners of the ground. The frustrated bowler starts to pitch short and our man puts the ball over the trees, into the road, and hits a passing car – a very nice looking car. The driver is later seen entering the clubhouse in a state of some distress and annoyance. He is deflated to receive the customary response: 'We were playing cricket here before the car was invented, so hard luck!'

Despite his usual quota of run-outs (only two on a good day) the lion-killer is still scoring quickly, and a bowling change is called for. A tall slow left-arm bowler takes over. Not having practised all season, we are treated by him to a series of full tosses – all dispatched. Searching for the ball is prolonged by the fielding side in the hope of using up time. The captain mischievously asks the bowler if the pitch is 'doing anything at all?' Eventually a line and length is found and the ball begins to spin – certain doom for our man at the crease.

Sure enough he soon gets a thick edge and is caught in the gully. Congratulations all round! But the batsman stands his ground. A huge belated appeal is answered in the affirmative by an old lady on the boundary, and later by me. The lion-killer leaves the scene at a funereal pace, dragging his bat. I know, though, that he will apologise later for this refusal to 'walk', and I shall receive a drink.

Such has been the assault on the bowling that only a few runs are required for a home win. However these are very slow in coming because of the desperate attempt by a middle-order player to push his 45 up to 50. One in an over, then a maiden, then another one, then another maiden. Finally there is a loud appeal from spectators on the boundary at what looks like a possible LBW and our player umpire, taken by surprise, gives him out. With him gone the match is quickly over.

I am thanked by the home side and ignored by the away team. When all is cleared away I get my hard-worked for 'fee' of one Diet Coke from the captain. See you all next week!

ROSS WALKER

10

Club Officers

Patron

1951–1965
Rt. Hon. Sir Winston Churchill, KG, OM, CH, MP

1970–1981
Col. Sir Stuart Mallinson, CBE, DSO, MC, DL, JP

President

1890	C. Keed
1919–1928	Sir Arthur E. Cutforth
1928–1939	E. E. Starke
1946–1951	Sir James A. Hawkey, Bart., JP
1952–1969	Col. Sir Stuart Mallinson
1970–79	P. F. N. Warner JP
1980–84	A. G. Waterman
1987–	A. G. Lindfield

Chairman

1919–	F. G. Knight
1946	J. Chumbley
1947	L. G. Allen
1948–1951	L. W. Powter
1952–1960	D. C. Bennett
1961–1962	R. I. Edwards
1963–1964	A. Beadham
1965–1969	J. G. Menote
1970–1973	B. D. Lewis
1974–1986	A. G. Lindfield
1987–1988	R. J. Palmer
1989–1993	F. R. Wolstenholme
1994–	R. C. Dodson

Vice-Chairman

1954–1960	R. I. Edwards
1961–1962	A. Beadham
1963–1964	R. I. Edwards
1965–1966	K. Carpenter
1967	G. D. Wood
1968–1969	B. D. Lewis
1970–1973	A. G. Lindfield
1974–1981	P. S. Howe
1982–1986	R. J. Palmer
1987–1988	B. G. Perring
1989–1991	J. Lindfield
1992–1993	P. G. Pearce
1994–1996	F. R. Wolstenholme
1997–1999	T. G. Spicer

Hon Secretary

1890	C. Jessop
1907	A. Stokes
1908–1914	J. Hill (*killed in action*)
1914–1918	Sam Tyler
1919–	A. B. Walls
	A. Stokes
	Jack Hill
1928	A. G. Wright
1933	S. W. Smith
1934–38	C. L. Arman
1938	H. Bourner
1946	H. Hancock
1947–1951	E. G. Gatcum
1952–1955	F. S. Croxon
1956–1957	A. Sheppard
1958–1963	G. C. Crawley
1964–1990	J. G. Lewis
1991–1996	A. Jethwa
1997	W. Naismith
1998–	D. A. V. Baker

Hon Treasurer

1890	C. Jessop
1919–1934	E. W. Barrett
1935	C. L. Arman
1946–1950	H. Dowle
1951–1955	H. J. Chick
1956–1958	L. H. G. Oldham
1959–1964	J. G. Menote
1965–1970	J. E. Andrews
1971–1985	A. Sheppard
1986–	R. C. Dodson

Hon Fixture Secretary

1938	H. Bourner
1946	C. H. Reason
1947–1948	E. Marriott
1949–1955	H. J. Chick
1956–1957	S. W. A. Richardson
1958–1961	H. J. Chick
1962–1966	J. C. Chumbley
1967	J. R. Knight
1968–1978	G. D. Wood
1979–1983	F. R. Wolstenholme
1984–1988	J. M. Evans
1989–1996	D. A. V. Baker
1997–	I. Fullbrook

Club Captain

1875–1903	William 'Blondin' Griggs
1904–1912	Joseph Mussett
1913–1914	Charlie Roper
1919	F. G. Knight
1925–1927	C. H. Sansom
1927	R. Burton
1946–47	S. Wright
1948–1949	R. I. Edwards
1950–1951	A. Swingler
1952	R. I. Edwards
1954	A. Sheppard

1955	R. I. Edwards
1956	J. G. Menote
1957–1958	G. D. Wood
1959–1960	P. S. Howe
1961	M. J. Curry
1962	J. E. Andrews
1963–1964	P. S. Howe
1961	M. J. Curry
1962	J. E. Andrews
1963–1964	P. S. Howe
1965	G. D. Wood
1966–1967	J. Smith-Pryor
1968	S. Richardson / P. S. Howe
1969	P. S. Howe

2nd XI Captain

1947–1949	J. Menote
1951	F. Croxon
1952	D. Jameson
1954–1957	A. G. Lindfield
1958	D. C. Bennett
1959	A. Beadham
1960	D. Anderson
1961	T. W. Dearsley
1962–1964	K. Carpenter
1965	A. G. Lindfield
1966	R. J. Palmer
1967–1968	J. R. Knight
1969	D. E. North
1970	J. Wright
1971	R. North

Saturday 1st XI Captain

1970–1973	B. G. Perring
1974–1978	R. Dodson
1979–1980	P. H. Crockford
1981–1983	C. Bunney
1984–1985	T. J. Ereira
1986–1988	A. Malcolm

1989	R. Newman
1990–1991	J. Bernard
1992	S. Newton
1993–1994	M. Taylor
1995–1996	M. Halford
1997	T. Spicer
1998	P. Nicholls
1999	R. Newman

Sunday A XI Captain

1970–1972	P. S. Howe
1973–1975	G. D. Wood
1976–1977	C. de Boer
1978	M. Curry
1979–1982	J. A. Lindfield
1983–1985	R. Newman
1986–1988	T. G. Spicer
1989	A. Malcolm / L. Newman
1990	L. Newman
1991	R. Newman
1992–1993	B. Grinham
1994	M. Bacchus
1995	A. Malcolm
1996–1998	W. Naismith
1999	M. Mukherjee

Saturday 2ND XI Captain

1972–1974	D. E. North
1975	R. V. Lawrence
1976	W. Dodd
1977	R. V. Lawrence
1978–1979	D. E. North
1980–1982	C. Mulligan
1983–1984	A. R. A. Rudelhoff
1985–1987	W. Naismith
1988	B. G. Perring
1989–1990	D. Gardiner
1991–1996	A. Jethwa
1997–	R. Locke

Sunday B XI Captain

1972	A. G. Lindfield
	D. A. V. Baker
	B. D. Lewis
1973–1975	D. A. V. Baker
1976–1982	J. E. Andrews
1983	P. E. Howe
1984–1985	P. Pearce
1986	C. Carter
1987–1989	J. Snowden
1990–1995	W. Naismith
1996	A. Naismith
1997–1998	C. Chin
1999	B. Ereira

Saturday 3RD XI Captain

1982	P. S. Howe
1983–1984	J. M. Evans
1985–1986	J. G. Lewis
1987–1988	B. J. Plume
1989–1990	J. Andrews
1991	T. Everett
1992–1995	B. Perring
1996	J. Desai
1997–	M. Davis

Sunday C XI Captain

1984	J. G. Lewis
1985–1987	A. Jethwa
1988	C. Chin
1989–1990`	J. G. Lewis
1991	W. Jetham
1992–1993	A. Lindfield
1994–1997	D. Rowlands
1998–	P. Shearman

Above: Woodford Green First XI, 1999.
Below: W.G.C.C. officers, 1999.
Next page: aerial view of the Green.

President:
A. G. LINDFIELD, Esq.
7 Aurora Court, 14a Sunset Avenue
Woodford Green, Essex IG8 0SN

Life Vice-President:
A. SHEPPARD, Esq.

Vice-Presidents:

J. ANDREWS, Esq.	D. A. V. BAKER, Esq.
Mrs. S. BAKER	D. C. BENNETT, Esq.
J. C. CHUMBLEY, Esq.	R. C. DODSON, Esq.
R. I. EDWARDS, Esq.	B. D. LEWIS, Esq.
Mrs. E. LINDFIELD	W. NAISMITH, Esq.
R. B. NEWMAN, Esq.	B. G. PERRING, Esq.
Mrs. S. SHEPPARD	F. R. WOLSTENHOLME, Esq.
G. D. WOOD, Esq.	

OFFICERS

Chairman and Hon. Treasurer:
R. C. DODSON
15 Fairlight Avenue
Woodford Green, Essex IG8 9JP

Vice-Chairman and Hon. Team Secretary:
T. G. SPICER
13 Rokeby Gardens
Woodford Green, Essex IG8 9HT

Hon. Secretary:
D. A. V. BAKER
21 Aston Court, Broomhill Road
Woodford Green, Essex IG8 9EY

Hon. Fixture Secretary:
I. FULLBROOK
13 Weale Road, Chingford, London E4 6JL

Hon. League Representative:
J. DESAI
31 Marlborough Road
Forest Gate, London E7 8HA

Hon. Membership Secretary:
Mrs. S. J. BAKER
21 Aston Court, Broomhill Road
Woodford Green, Essex IG8 9EY

Hon. Colts Secretary:
D. A. COATES
131 Grosvenor Drive, Loughton, Essex IG10 2LB